Mahler

Mahler

Henry Raynor

The Musicians

General Editor: Geoffrey Hindley

M

To Ivor Newton for friendship and music

Half-title page: *Mahler in 1902, etching by Orlik.*
Mahler was often photographed but there are very
few Mahler portraits
Title page: '*The God of the Southern Regions*'.
Mahler in his office at the Vienna Imperial Opera

© Macmillan London Ltd. 1975

SBN 333 14579 8

Picture research by Susan Bower

First published 1975 by
Macmillan London Limited
London and Basingstoke
Associated companies in New York, Toronto,
Dublin, Melbourne, Johannesburg and Delhi

Filmset by BAS Printers Limited
Over Wallop, Hampshire
Printed in Great Britain by Waterlow (Dunstable) Ltd.

Contents

Chapter 1

A Posthumous Triumph

'In forty or fifty years, they won't be playing Beethoven's symphonies,' said Gustav Mahler, Director of the Vienna Opera, to Max Graf, a young music critic. 'Mine will have taken their place.' Whenever the performance of one of his works ended in as much booing as cheering or he became aware of a critical attack on his work, he simply said 'My time will come.' Touched and delighted by critical understanding and sympathy, he paid no attention to anything that was said against him. Sardonically he referred to the critics as 'our superiors' and explained to his wife that his enemies were 'the immature and the Philistines'. As a conductor, he was convinced of his total fidelity, not to the score he played—he explained that the most important things about any music are not in the notes—but to its composer's intentions, divined through careful study and gruelling rehearsal. As a composer, he had complete faith in everything he wrote; to him it was the result of transcendental inspiration worked out by consummate technique. 'A man like me, born with a destined mission, cannot be led astray either by unjust criticism or by empty praise.'

'My time will come' was not a brave response to neglect and empty halls. From 1894, when he conducted his First Symphony at Weimar, until 1910, when for the last time he conducted the first performance of one of his works, guiding a multitude of singers and players through the Eighth Symphony in the newly-built Musikfesthalle, in Munich, his works provided sensational excitement. From the first, Mahler and his music were adored or detested; the first performance of his Fourth Symphony in Vienna, in 1902, saw the warmest, happiest and most companionable of his symphonies end in a fight between rival factions in the audience. What his time was to bring when it came, according to his own reckoning, in the 1940s or 1950s, was not excited attention but total acceptance. It would not be a series of explosive excitements, once heard and then put aside, but would belong to the repertory because it would be recognized to be as important, as moving and as life-enhancing as anything by his adored Beethoven or Wagner. He was convinced that he had been sent into the world to interpret life and human experience: the time would come when the validity of his interpretation was universally recognized.

Mahler lived a life of furious activity. He was one of the supreme conductors of his period, but he left destiny to look after his own affairs. He never made it his business to impose his own compositions on the world or to win a place in the repertory for them though it would have been easy for him to live as a star conductor, travelling with a handful of programmes which invariably included a work of his own. After his death in 1911, Samuel Langford, the first English music critic to understand Mahler's originality and importance, drew attention to Mahler's unwillingness to push his music into prominence:

He was to an extraordinary degree accessory to his own neglect, inasmuch as he but rarely used his power and influence to procure the performance of his own work. His music is probably all the better and more pure in style for that indifference.

In another respect, too, Mahler was his own worst enemy. His symphonies exist on a vast time scale and demand large orchestras in which each member plays music of great complexity, particularly in regard to balance. His orchestra, so to speak, is a vast chamber music ensemble in which each instrument, from the double bass to the piccolo, has to face a passage in which it carries important musical significance. Leaving aside the Fourth Symphony, which according to its title-page is for 'small orchestra' but which needs more players than any symphony by Beethoven and lasts for nearly an hour, none of his symphonies lasts for less than an hour or fails to demand quadruple wood-wind, six or eight horns and trumpets and a large battery of

6

The Medal of Honour of the Bruckner–Mahler Society of America, presented to musicians and writers who further the cause of those two composers

percussion, even when it does not ask for post horns, mandoline, cowbells, a harmonium, bells and other eccentric additions to the standard orchestra. To his unusual musical demands for exactitude of balance in a new style he added the problems of music on an extravagantly extensive scale; with the needs for extra rehearsal and extra players, Mahler performances were therefore expensive, rare and not often convincing.

Whatever was unusual about Mahler's style and musical vocabulary grew from his conception of the nature of the symphony, and this was entirely alien to the ideas of his time. 'A symphony should be like the world,' he said to Sibelius (a composer whose music he detested but whose company he enjoyed). 'It should contain everything.' In one of his letters he wrote, 'Symphony, to me, means using all the available techniques to build a world.' This idea from the start baffled or outraged some of Mahler's contemporaries. To them a symphony was a fundamentally serious expression of a single complex of experiences; Brahms had explained that a symphony is no joke. Mahler's determination to co-ordinate all the diversities of his unusually complex world of varied experiences and emotions in order to force them into relationship, openly challenged the intellectual current of his day.

For Mahler, to find the music that expressed these diversities was not difficult: his world encompasses not only intensities of expression but wide extremes of emotion. He expresses exalted serenity, ungovernable joy, unendurable tragedy, wild irony, savage anger, bitter derision, harsh jeering and cosy, easy-going sentimentality in tunes as familiarly turned as folk song. Among the many unconventional directions which appear in his scores are *mit humor*, *mit parodie*, *grob* (roughly) and *keck* (cheekily). His aim was to write symphonies in which all these mutually exclusive states of being and modes of expression should achieve their proper place and relationship to each other; those who find his music intolerable cannot understand, or cannot accept, the idea of a musical world embracing all these diversities, some of which seem to them to be hardly worth the labour of expressing. That is why a critic like Ernst Roth could write:

One cannot say irrelevant things with grand gestures in a grand manner.

The unsympathetic critic was affronted not only by the range of Mahlerian experience and emotion, but still more by the passages which seemed to be of less than true symphonic dignity—moments of easy relaxation, folksy cheerfulness or sentiment and frankly popular appeal. The *Musical Courier*, of New York, discussed the Fourth Symphony in 1902, very soon after its first performance. Perhaps it is surprising that so frankly appealing a work should have infuriated the critic but the author of the *Musical Courier*'s notice concentrated his sense of outrage on the variations of the slow movement, which gather speed and gaiety:

The *Adagio* is harmless enough; but suddenly we are introduced to a circus scene. That may be a not unwelcome diversion for some; but without wishing to be traditional or pedantic, we cannot but remark that for us it was a shock and an unpleasant one.

The writer goes on to suggest that 'portions of the Adagio' could be used by pleasure steamers on the Danube.

Two years later the *Musical Courier* sent another critic to hear the Fourth Symphony. He sat down to write, bitter from his experience of 'the drooling and emasculated simplicity of Gustav Mahler' and at having borne 'one hour or more of the most painful musical torture' from 'that musical monstrosity which masquerades under the title of Mahler's Fourth Symphony.' There is, it seems, a strong strain of puritanism, outraged by sentiment and popularity of style, in early objections to Mahler's works.

Mahler admitted into his symphonies themes and melodies at which many composers, as well as the critics themselves, superciliously turned up their noses. But since 'it takes all sorts to make a world', it takes all sorts of experiences to make a Mahler symphony. For Mahler, with nerves situated abnormally close to the skin, was susceptible to a wider range of feeling than most people, and felt even commonplace emotions with extreme intensity. The only quality his music seems to lack is eroticism; none of his themes are musical endearments and caresses like so many of those which move us most deeply in Tchaikovsky's orchestral scores.

There were Austrian and German critics who decided that Mahler's Jewish birth was enough to explain the features of his work which they found objectionable. Such writers had dutifully studied Wagner's *Judaism in Music* which, at its nearest to sanity, explains that the Jewish

Gustav Mahler in 1892, at the time of his only conducting engagement in London

8

composers with whose work Wagner was familiar—notably Mendelssohn, Meyerbeer and Halévy—having no national tradition of art music, wrote with, so to speak, a foreign accent. In 1909, Rudolf Louis applied the Wagnerian doctrine to Mahler:

If Mahler's music spoke Yiddish I would, perhaps, find it incomprehensible. What I find repulsive about it is that it *acts* Yiddish. That is, it speaks German, but with the accent, the inflection and, more than anything else, the gesticulations of an all-too-Eastern Jew. But nobody has to be repelled by Mahler's musical personality to realise the emptiness, the complete vacuity, of an art in which spasms of would-be Titanesque grandeur turn out to be nothing more than the emotional satisfactions of a sentimental seamstress.

Louis, like the American writers, finds the most offensive thing about Mahler's music to be its moments of popular, easy-going sentiment within a form which, according to received ideas, should be at every moment serious and elevated in style. Mahler's use of the most savage dissonances, the counterpoints launched on inevitable collision courses—these things do not, apparently, worry him any more than the fact that Mahler's harmony, for much of the time, is motivated by the interaction of two or three contrapuntal lines of equal thematic significance. Such unorthodoxies, like the 'progressive tonality' which opens a work in one key and ends it in another, passed without any yells of critical rage.

But even a relatively sympathetic writer, Richard Aldrich, music critic of *The New York Times* from 1902–23, who wrote enthusiastically of Mahler the conductor, had his doubts about the value of Mahler's compositions. When, in April 1916, Leopold Stokowski repeated in New York the performance of Mahler's Eighth Symphony which had been a triumphant success in Philadelphia, Aldrich wrote:

All Mahler's symphonies have occasioned renewed and heightened interest—an interest that has not always been maintained at so high a pitch after they have been made known.

It would be 'unjust', Aldrich admitted, to attribute the excitement caused by Stokowski's performance simply to the vast scale of the Eighth; the work contains 'great incidental beauties; Mahler's themes are usually forcible and direct in their line.' But they are 'submitted to the rack and thumbscrew of mordantly dissonant harmonies, are broken and tortured relentlessly.'

It is not really easy to see in this composer the really potent achievement of a creative imagination. It seems rather the high aspiration of a musician of great skill and knowledge, of far-reaching intelligence, intense earnestness and truly spiritual promptings; a musician whose lofty ambitions are not matched by his inspiration.

By this time, the grounds for uncertainty were shifting their base from the cheapness and sentimentality of some of Mahler's themes to the larger idea of the doubtful quality of his inspiration.

In January, 1913, *The Times* prepared its readers for Henry Wood's performance of the Seventh Symphony—the first English performance—in an article 'The Symphonies of Gustav Mahler'; this guaranteed to keep from the hall any reader susceptible to the influence of music critics. Its author noted the finesse and precision of Mahler's orchestration, but nothing else pleased him:

Whatever we may think of the musical ideas of the First Symphony, and the best that can be said of them is that they are infantile in their simplicity, there was no doubt that he believed in them and thought them strong enough to bear all the weight which a big scheme involving much repetition and a big orchestra throws upon them . . . This faith in himself made him treat his own trivial ideas with an absurd seriousness, yet along with it went a certain humour which sometimes succeeded in making his hearers suppose him to be serious when he was laughing, for he was like a man who makes a little joke in a sonorous bass voice and without a twinkle. Such a man has no right to complain if he is voted a bore.

One wonders on what evidence the critic, still clearly in the first stage of Anti-Mahlerism decided that the Eighth Symphony 'has a nobility which has no parallel in his earlier work.' The Eighth Symphony was, in 1913, almost completely unknown.

Ernest Newman, few of whose thoughts about Mahler have survived, wrote about Wood's performance of the Seventh as though he had really been able to hear what was happening, while other critics seemed less lucky.

What struck me was . . . the exquisite balance between the means and the end, the perfect certainty both of Mahler's thinking and of his style. One can hardly imagine a composer more sure of himself in latitudes not accessible to ordinary feet.

Above: Mahler and his supporters in Amsterdam. The second conductor of the Concertgebouw Orchestra, Cornelius Dopper, is standing behind Mahler. Willem Mengelberg is on Dopper's right and the composer Alphons Diepenbrock to the right of Mengelberg

Little was heard about the doubtfulness of Mahler's inspiration, for little was heard of Mahler's music, for some years. When, in 1920, Willem Mengelberg mounted a Mahler Festival at which all the symphonies were played, Samuel Langford was the only English critic to write of it at length as an important musical event. Even continental critics regarded it coolly; one German writer announcing with some relief that a Mahler Festival having been held, no Mahler Festival would ever be necessary in the future. The second stage in Mahler criticism nevertheless arrived at length with the BBC's performance of the Eighth Symphony, which the indefatigable Wood conducted in 1930. The BBC prepared for this as a major event, printing in the programmes of the public concerts earlier in the season a study of the work by Ernest Newman, whose enthusiasm for the Seventh Symphony seems not to have extended to the Eighth. Newman saw Mahler as:

One of the really curious paradoxes in all music— that of a truly original mind failing, to some extent, to make an original instrument for the expression of itself.

The reader feels that questions are being begged; what, in this context, is originality? Mahler's synthesis of contrary styles into a unified whole, his fundamentally contrapuntal turn of mind, the daring of his harmonic vocabulary and the fine drawn precision and delicacy of his orchestration were unlike anything else of which Newman was aware, but they seemed not to count as originality.

To the modern listener, of course, Mahler's music sounds remarkably direct and explicit; to look for hidden meanings when a direct meaning is so clearly stated seems to be a mysterious but foolish waste of time; no composer worked harder than Mahler to be explicit, but critics unfamiliar with his thought processes and idoms naturally found it easy to miss the point. But, the *Times* critic might have continued, we are not puzzled by hidden meanings in the works of Haydn, Mozart, Beethoven and Brahms, therefore 'inspired' music can be taken at its face value. The notion that he might have developed a personal style not immediately within their grasp seems to have been beyond the critics. So it seemed that Mahler's music lacked 'inspiration' and the fact that the composer himself claimed inspiration for it could mean no more than that Mahler was, pen in

Below: Mahler and Alma Mahler (front row, right) with friends after the first performance in Amsterdam of the Fifth Symphony and the Kindertotenlieder

hand, incurably self-deluding.

Thus the almost unplayed composer ceased to be a monster of cheap, sentimental sensationalism and became a monster of another sort. His themes ceased to be sentimental, banal, vulgar; they were discovered to be the creations of a monster of uninspired intelligence who put together enormous symphonies with a powerful intellectual grip, no genuine 'inspiration' and very doubtful taste. Even his orchestration (which reveals itself as remarkably original to anybody who bothers to look at a Mahler score) was discovered to be dull, grey and muddled. It is hard to believe that many of the critics who dismissed Mahler in the 1920s and '30s made any effort to discover the facts with which they were supposed to be dealing. Those who lamented the heavy dullness of Mahler's orchestration needed only to look at the scores to notice the space and ventilation that are the real nature of his orchestral style, the result of an insatiable appetite for complete clarity.

From the intellectualism and dullness of sound discovered in these works, it was only a step to the discovery of Mahler's morbid gloominess. The critics of the '20s and '30s decided that Mahler had one mood, not elevated enough to be called tragic: his music, we read, is simply morbid, wallowing with unhealthy insistence in self-pity and dwelling with sick insistence on misery.

Of course, Mahler's principles admit self-pity, as they admit all emotion and experience; there are passages in the symphonies which delight in self-pity. But the First, Second, Fifth and Seventh symphonies end in triumph; the Fourth ends in childlike delight, the Third in rapturous serenity, the Eighth in religious ecstasy. Only the Sixth ends in appalled hopelessness, for *Das Lied von der Erde* and the Ninth Symphony achieve a heart-breaking reconciliation with death; the end of *Das Lied* is a passionate recognition not of pain and loss but of the continuing beauty of the world and human life. The attack on Mahler's emotional limitations, like the attack on his dullness, comes from ignorance.

The further Mahler's time receded, the more completely his cause seemed to be lost. When the Second World War ended, only two of his symphonies—the Fourth and the Ninth—were available on gramophone records with the *Adagietto* of the Fifth.

It was, perhaps, the advent of the long-

GUSTAV MAHLER'S EIGHTH SYMPHONY BROADCAST FROM THE QUEEN'S HALL

Conducted by SIR HENRY J. WOOD
in the 21st and last Concert of the Season

Magna Peccatrix ...	...	ELSIE SUDDABY
Una Poenitentium ...	...	...MAY BLYTH
Mater Gloriosa ...	...	IRENE MORDEN
Mulier Samaritana...		MURIEL BRUNSKILL
Maria Ægyptiaca ...	...	CLARA SERENA
Doctor Marianus ...		...WALTER WIDDOP
Pater Ecstaticus ...		HAROLD WILLIAMS
Pater Profundus ...	...	ROBERT EASTON

THE NATIONAL CHORUS
Chorus Master, Stanford Robinson

A CHORUS OF BOYS
Choristers from Southwark Cathedral; Holy Trinity, Sloane Square; St. Stephen's, Wallbrook; and the Alexandra Orphanage

THE B.B.C. SYMPHONY ORCHESTRA
Principal Violin, Arthur Catterall

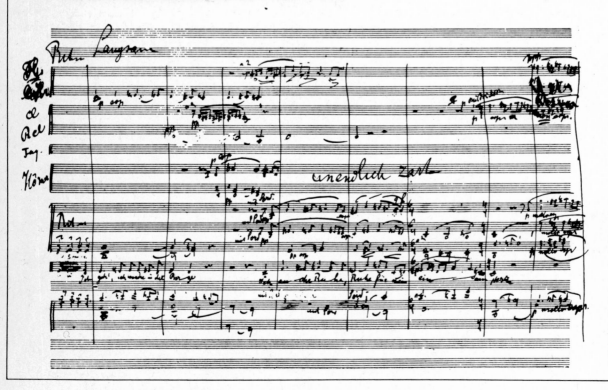

Above: Announcement in The Listener *of the first English performance of Mahler's Eighth Symphony on April 15th 1930*

Left: 'I go, I wander in the mountains. I look for rest for my lonely heart.' Facsimile of Mahler's autograph of a passage from Der Abschied, *the last movement of* Das Lied von der Erde

playing record which changed the situation. By the beginning of the 1950s, the whole accepted repertoire existed in rival or duplicate versions on LPs; the market was expanding, and there was room for new music on disc, to be heard and assimilated by listeners in their homes, so Mahler was slowly explored. Soon, Mahler conductors and Mahler singers had multiplied extraordinarily; an insatiable appetite for Mahler's music in the United States and Britain created Mahlerian performers enough to carry their gospel back into Europe, where Mahlerian ideas and principles had been lost since Germany had banned the music of Jewish composers. Mahler's time had come.

Fashions, of course, are never simply fashions; they have a reason. The music we neglect is that which is irrelevant to our concerns, and whatever other virtues it may possess, without that relevance we care nothing for it. Why, in the 1960s, did we discover that the music of a Bohemian-Jewish-Catholic-

pantheist-mystic with nerves abnormally exposed to all experience and emotion was not only relevant to our experience but necessary to our musical well-being?

Mahler composed to find the unity and the reality in the crowded, contradictory experience and emotions of a vigorous, stormy life made difficult by his own personality. In reality and unity, he believed, he would find the serenity and peace which, to him, were manifestations of God. In a sense, everything he wrote is an episode in a vast biographical-religious-philosophical work. His time has come; his apparently self-deluded, boastful prophecy has been fulfilled at a time when it is difficult for his audiences to see their own experience as anything but uncoordinated, contradictory, lacking in unity and meaning, and also pitifully fragmented. The Mahler-lover of today is not simply exploring a sixty-year-old idiom; he is finding the music which suggests that the fragments of his own unsatisfactory experience can be resolved into unity and meaning.

Chapter 2

Father to the Man

Gustav Mahler, who thought in such terms as these, might well have believed that Nature seemed to go out of her way to ensure him a hard life. She endowed him with creative genius and added to it the interpretative power of a great conductor. To be sure that these rich gifts did not sustain and complement each other, she planted in him a longing for solitariness and peace together with a passion for action and an urge to dominate and overrule. She sent him through life with a craving for friendship mocked by an inborn conviction that consideration for others would entail compromise and would therefore betray the mission with which he was entrusted. He could not have friendship on equal terms; all those closest to him were to be disciples.

The conflicts in his personality were echoed by those of his situation. A sensitive, acutely intelligent adolescent living in Vienna could not fail to notice that as a Bohemian Jew, a citizen of the Austrian empire born close to the Moravian border in an area passionate for national independence, he was, nationally speaking, everything and nothing. To add another complication, the Jewish enclaves in Bohemia, where he grew up, were German rather than Austrian in culture and way of life. Vienna, where his most crucial years were spent, was the most anti-semitic of cities. As a Jew, he belonged to a race for centuries denied entry into most areas of Central-European life, which had survived by sheer fortitude in the face of a system which condemned them to poverty. Mahler shared precarious health and an over-tense nervous system with his brothers and sisters, but he suffered an incurable sense of homelessness. As a middle-aged man, he explained to his wife:

I am thrice homeless: as a Bohemian in Austria, as an Austrian among Germans, and as a Jew throughout all the world. Everywhere an intruder, never welcomed.

'My life is one long homesickness,' he said. In Vienna, Mahler may have been specially conscious of his fate as a born outsider. The city was beautiful and offered a certain graciousness of life, but the Austrian Empire in decline left its people purposeless, self-satisfied and frivolously complacent. They loved the music they knew and the way of life into which they had been born, but though Vienna was the real centre of Mahler's existence, he could never share Viennese *Gemütlichkeit* or lapse into Viennese complacency; the city he loved best acted on him as he acted on it—as an irritant.

Mahler, divided against himself and at odds with life, was the child of a bitterly divided family. He was born at Kaliste in Bohemia in 1860, apparently on 7 July, the date given on his birth certificate, though his family kept 1 July as his birthday. His father, Bernard Mahler, who was then thirty-three years old, was a violent, harsh-tempered man, passionately ambitious for education and social advancement. He married above his class when he chose Marie Hermann, the daughter of a reasonably well-to-do soap-maker. Perhaps the fact that Marie was sickly and lame made it possible for Bernard to take her off her parents' hands. The son of a street pedlar, he began life as a carter and at times earned his living as a factory worker though he was to rise to salaried status as a private tutor. Marie Hermann was in love with another man, who apparently hardly noticed her existence, and the marriage was without affection on either side. He was hot-tempered, brutal, fiercely energetic; she was quiet, incapable of self-defence, and spiritless. Gustav inherited the most violently opposed characteristics of them both.

Despite Marie's lameness and heart-disease, the pair had twelve children, five of whom died in infancy: Gustav was the eldest of the survivors. His sisters, Justine and Emma, who kept house for him after their parents' death, both eventually married talented musicians. His

Below: His mother, Marie

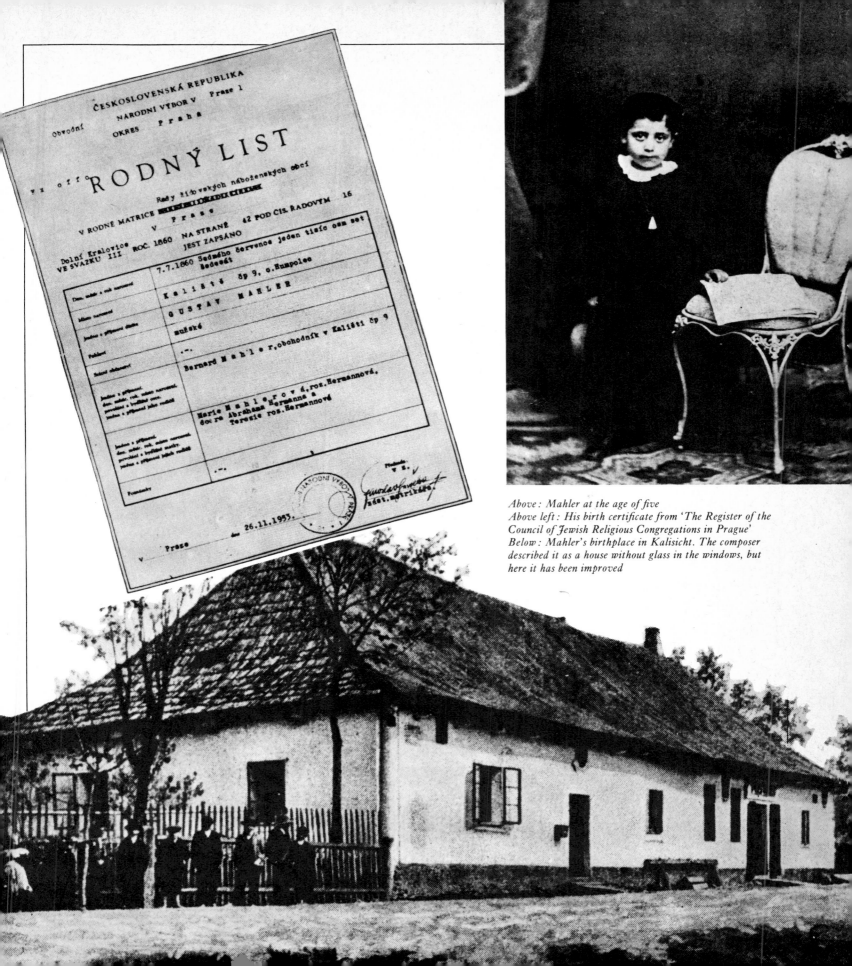

Above: Mahler at the age of five
Above left: His birth certificate from 'The Register of the Council of Jewish Religious Congregations in Prague'
Below: Mahler's birthplace in Kalisicht. The composer described it as a house without glass in the windows, but here it has been improved

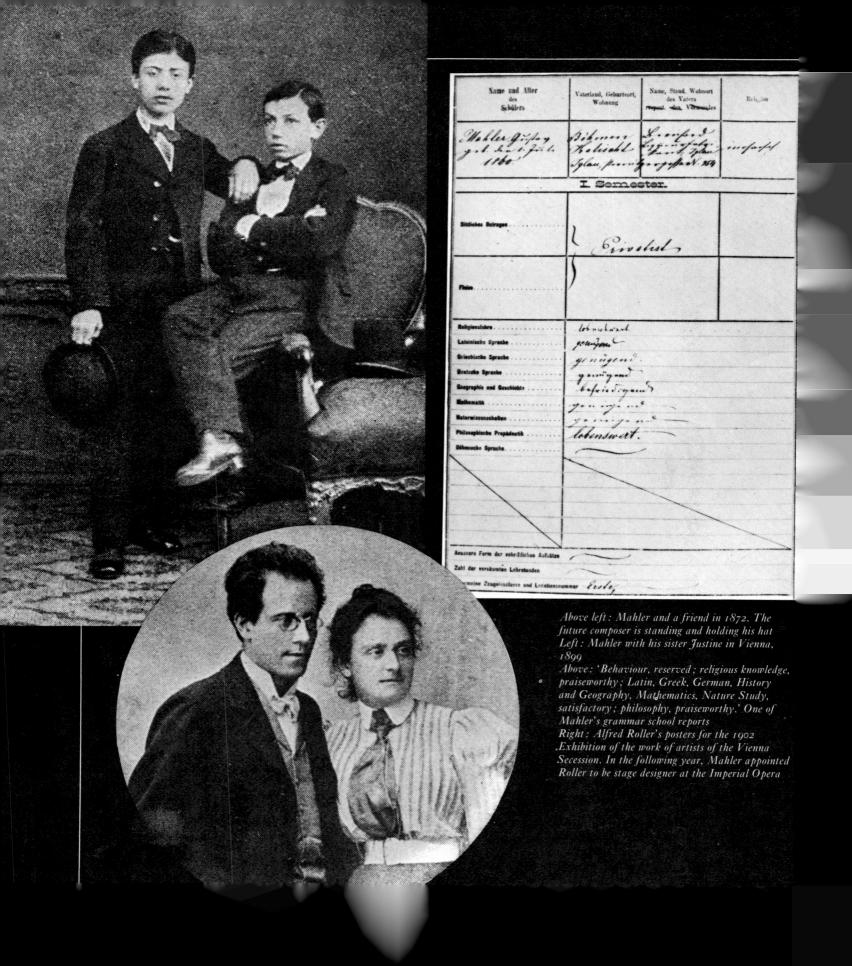

Above left: Mahler and a friend in 1872. The future composer is standing and holding his hat

Left: Mahler with his sister Justine in Vienna, 1899

Above: 'Behaviour, reserved; religious knowledge, praiseworthy; Latin, Greek, German, History and Geography, Mathematics, Nature Study, satisfactory; philosophy, praiseworthy.' One of Mahler's grammar school reports

Right: Alfred Roller's posters for the 1902 Exhibition of the work of artists of the Vienna Secession. In the following year, Mahler appointed Roller to be stage designer at the Imperial Opera

brother Alois, who called himself 'Hans' in order to sound less Jewish, was an unsatisfactory young man living on distant terms with reality. He convinced himself, but failed to convince the world, of his impressive family background, status as a man of fashion (he dressed the part in spite of his very limited means), and his intellectual power. He was an irritating embarrassment, and Gustav seems to have felt nothing but relief when he ran away to America to escape imprisonment after forging bank notes to pay his debts.

Otto, born when Gustav was thirteen, was a promising musician; Gustav taught him and drilled him through his school examinations, found him minor posts in Austrian theatres and remained patient and affectionate when Otto left them one after one from lack of confidence and idleness. In 1895, at the age of twenty-two, leaving behind him a trunk full of compositions which Gustav never found courage to examine, Otto wrote a note to say that 'Life no longer pleased him so he had returned his ticket', and shot himself.

Mahler's favourite was his brother Ernst, born in 1861 and therefore nearest in age as well as affection to the future composer. Ernst's death at the age of thirteen was a blow from which Gustav seems never to have recovered. His first major work, *Das klagende Lied*, is based on a fairy tale of the murder of a sister; but Mahler changed this into the murder of a brother and then performed and published the work with the first section, the story of the murder, omitted; later Mahler, the famous father of two adored little girls, set Rückert's poems about the death of his children to music as the *Kindertotenlieder*. It was as if he remained convinced that because Ernst died, beloved children are born only to die.

When Gustav was five, Bernard became the owner of a small distillery (apparently only a grand name for a drink shop) in Iglau, because in that year the Jews were at last allowed to move freely about Austria. The 'distillery' must have been poor enough, but apparently it rescued the Mahlers from the abysmal poverty in which they had lived at Kalisch in a cottage without glass for its windows. In Iglau, the Mahler children had a nursemaid of sorts, who took the child for walks past the neighbouring barracks; the trumpet calls and military music, which were to haunt his compositions, impressed themselves indelibly on his mind.

In Iglau the children grew up, terrified of their father, abnormally sensitive, morbidly imaginative, never out of the firing line in the war between their savage father and their quiescent, helpless mother whose passivity seems to have been a stimulus to Bernard's brutalities. All the children were incapable of facing reality and suffered from a sense of inevitable tragedy. Justine 'stuck candles all round the edge of her cot. Then she lay down and lit the candles and firmly believed that she was dead.' Gustav himself, when asked what he intended to be when he grew up, answered 'a martyr'.

Over and over again Mahler's music shatters a mood of tragedy with noisy, cheap music in a way that is strangely harsh and disturbing. Gustav was only a tiny child when he ran out of the house to escape a particularly ferocious quarrel between his parents and heard a barrel organ churning out the Viennese popular song *O du lieber Augustin* in the street outside. This was a story he told to no one until, in 1910, determined if he could to save the marriage which he had nearly destroyed, he consulted Sigmund Freud and mentioned it to him. But he explained to others that he found tragedy always indissolubly mixed with triviality and that for him, tragic music seemed to demand interruption by cheap, meaningless tunes.

The trumpet calls and military music of the barracks, *O du lieber Augustin* and two hundred or more folk songs learned from the servants and their friends, were the music that became his repertory when at the age of four he was given an accordion. At about the same time he discovered a piano in the attic of his grandparents' house; when his father and mother finally tracked him down he was at the keyboard, trying to work out for himself the fundamentals of piano playing.

Bernard, regarding his son's passion for music as another possible way of family advancement, encouraged the boy. At six, Gustav began piano lessons first with the music director of the theatre in Iglau and then with a teacher named Brosch. His greatest friend at that time was the son of the church choirmaster; the young Mahler attended choir practices and services listening, absorbed, to the masses of Haydn, Mozart and Rossini. At the age of eight he belonged to a music circulating library and even had a pupil of his own—aged seven. When he was ten, his father arranged a concert for

Above left: The Belvedere Palace in Vienna
Left: Attersee. A painting by Klimpt who was a friend and contemporary of Mahler

him; he won flattering notices from the local papers and found himself in demand as a soloist and accompanist at local concerts. He played music by Schubert, Schumann, Chopin, Mendelssohn and Liszt, and the operatic fantasies made popular by Liszt and other virtuoso pianists in those days.

When he was eleven, his father took him away from the local Gymnasium (grammar school) and sent him to Prague to live in the house of new piano teachers, Alfred Grünfeld and his son Heinrich. Gustav's clothes and shoes were taken from him to be worn by other pupils; he was badly fed, dirty and neglected. Inadvertently he was a witness of what his wife (to whom alone he told the story) described as 'a brutal love scene between the servant and the son of the house'. Thinking that the girl was being attacked, he tried to defend her, and was startled to receive abuse instead of thanks. 'This little episode', wrote Alma Mahler 'left a deep mark on his mind'.

Bernard heard of the boy's condition only through rumours, but he immediately went to the rescue of the son on whom his hopes were fixed. Gustav had accepted his treatment with complete passivity, as though it were natural and inevitable; his mother suffered, so he should suffer too. It was the first sign of identification with his mother's suffering which he seems to have made subconsciously throughout his life. For example, although there seems to have been nothing physically wrong with his left leg, he always walked jerkily, dragging it as though it was necessary for him to walk as his mother walked.

This submission to circumstances points to another of his strange inconsistencies. As a practising musician he showed an indomitable will; neither his frail health nor the opposition of singers and orchestras ever deflected him from his goal. In other matters, he was almost totally passive. Just as he made very little effort to bring his music to public notice, so he made little effort to maintain himself in his official appointments. When his position as Director of the Vienna Imperial Opera hung in the balance and could easily have been preserved, he told Bruno Walter that he was 'making no resistance', and left events to take their course. While he fought for music with all his strength, he trusted providence to direct his life.

From childhood, music was his fulfilment; dreams were his escape from an intolerable

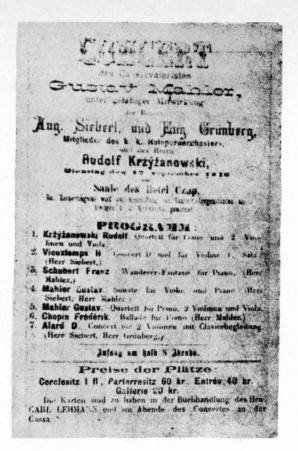

Left: This programme is of a concert given in Iglau by Mahler during his student days in the 1870s. It includes a quartet by his friend and fellow student Rudolf Kryzanowski, and the Violin Sonata which he later suppressed

world he refused to face directly. Fearing and hating his father, adoring his ill-treated mother and working at music gave him as much as he could cope with. He retreated from all other demands into dreamy quiescence, a habit reflected in his school reports and by a number of anecdotes which show that throughout his life he could always withdraw from his surroundings. When they were walking one day in the woods his father, remembering something left behind at home, ordered the boy to wait for him and promised to return soon. Bernard was delayed for several hours and when he returned, the boy was still sitting happily where he had been left, his mind far away. In school he would forget his surroundings and lose himself in his own world. When he began whistling snatches of melody he was soon brought back to the world of reality by the angry teacher.

Many examples of his abstraction, not to say absent-mindedness, come from later life. Natalie Bauer-Lechner, a friend of Mahler's from his conservatoire days and a notable violinist, appointed herself the Boswell of the years before his marriage; she remembered him, in a cafe, stirring his coffee with a cigarette

Above: Natalie Bauer-Lechner, the close friend of Gustav and Justine Mahler. From the beginning of his career until his marriage, she kept a careful record of Mahler's habits, opinions and conversations

the time, arranged to have the boy admitted after he had heard him play. Apparently half of Gustav's fees were remitted or Epstein arranged to pay them himself. A year later Mahler himself was compelled to ask for a further reduction of fees.

Departure to Vienna did not mean an immediate break with the tragic family relationships. These would undoubtedly have crippled him psychologically had he not found a way through music to order and redeem his experience. He continued to visit Iglau until his parents died in 1889, and actually appeared there as a guest conductor in 1882. Bernard Mahler, whether from love or ambition, had done all for his son that a poor man could do, but none of Mahler's confidants, not even his wife, reports a single affectionate or grateful word for the father. His mother and his dead brother Ernst seem to have exhausted his capacity for family love, though after Bernard and Marie died, he cared dutifully for his sisters and his brother Otto. His mother remained his ideal of what a woman should be. When, at the age of forty-two, he married Alma Maria Schindler, a girl half his age, beautiful, cultured, high-spirited and gifted, he told her that he was sorry her face was not 'stricken'. In Mahler's world true beauty was only to be found in faces marked by suffering.

Mahler's conservatoire course included piano, harmony and composition; because of the standard of his compositions, he was excused the classes in counterpoint which would have brought him into immediate contact with Anton Bruckner, who became his friend later. He won prizes for piano (1875–6 and 1876–7) and for composition with the first movement of a Piano Quartet (1876–7). At least the first movement of a Symphony was rehearsed at the Conservatoire, and the Scherzo of the Piano Quartet was played at a Students' Concert in 1878. Among a number of other works was a Piano Quintet which somehow survived his destruction of all his early music and has been played in recent years. When he matriculated in 1876 he began attending the university lectures in philosophy and also the music lectures of Anton Bruckner. Mahler's student years in Vienna were like those of the 'Bohemians' of Puccini's opera, a Bohemianism with the glamour rubbed off. His life was one of grinding poverty. He shared a room, and sometimes a bed, with Hugo Wolf, and like Wolf he

which he then attempted to smoke, spluttering coffee through it into the face of a woman sitting nearby. Walter remembered a rehearsal in Hamburg when, while the producer was dealing with some detail of stage movement, Mahler entirely forgot his surroundings. When he was recalled to business, he had completely forgotten where he was and yelled, 'Waiter, bring me my bill.'

Mahler never found it hard to keep reality at a safe distance or to see it as he wished it to be rather than as it actually was. Paul Stefan recalled a conversation in which Mahler was made angry by the suggestion that the thoughts in a shepherd's mind were probably about next market day. A shepherd, he replied, lives with nature and surely his mind is above material trivialities.

Such other worldliness and withdrawal from reality stemmed from his appalling childhood; in many other ways Mahler the child was unmistakably and tragically the father of the man. He was fifteen when his father managed to get him enrolled (1875) as a student at Vienna Conservatoire, where Julius Epstein, the best-known of the Conservatoire piano teachers at rebelled against the academic constrictions of Conservatoire music, though unlike Wolf he drew back from the dangerous step of ending his course before he had completed it. Other close friends were Anton Krisper and Hans Rott, for whom he felt a deep affinity. Rott became insane and died young and Mahler feared that Krisper, too, would lose his sanity. The atmosphere of strain and hysteria which Mahler had known at home continued.

He and his friends had to make what money they could by giving piano lessons. When absolute necessity demanded immediate money, one of them would ease the situation by calling on the parents of his most long-standing pupil, explaining that he was leaving Vienna and asking to be paid: the situation was saved at the cost of a pupil. Once when Mahler was working on his prize-winning Piano Quartet, Wolf and a fellow student, Heinrich Kryzanovsky, who was sharing their room at the time, left him undisturbed, spending the night on a bench in the Ringstrasse; at other times Mahler did as much for them. They found themselves thrown out, even from these unsatisfactory lodgings, thanks indirectly to Wagner. Returning from a performance of *Götterdämmerung*, 'they bawled the Gunther-Brünnhilde-Hagen trio (from Act Two) to such effect that their landlady came up in a fury and gave them notice on the spot. She would not leave the room till they had picked up their scanty belongings, and then she locked the door behind them'.

Wagner swept the young Mahler off his feet— as a thinker as well as composer. The revolutionary novelty of Wagner's music and the composer's lengthy, incessant dissertations on life, art, religion, philosophy and politics fell like a revelation on Mahler's willing ears in spite of their author's illogicalities, occasional absurdities, obsessions and even his increasingly scurrilous anti-semitism. When Wagner announced his conversion to vegetarianism in one of his *Bayreuther Blätter* pamphlets in October 1880, Mahler immediately became his fellow-convert, and within a month of reading

An engraving of the Ringstrasse in Vienna as Mahler knew it during his Conservatoire days

Wagner's words he wrote to his friend Emil Freund:

A month ago I became a complete vegetarian. The moral effect of this way of life—a voluntary subjugation of the body and its ever-increasing demands—is immense. You can understand how completely convinced I am by it when I tell you that through it I expect the regeneration of the human race.

Anton Bruckner made a more ambiguous impression on the young Mahler. Ridiculed for the novelty of his symphonic style by all except devout Wagnerians, who adopted him as the 'progressive' symphonist and their answer to the 'reactionary' Brahms, Bruckner had left his provincial organ loft in 1869, when he was forty-four, to become professor of the organ and of theory at the Vienna Conservatoire. Yet despite the difference in their ages, and despite the disastrous first performance of Bruckner's Third Symphony in 1877, when the audience simply laughed at the work, Mahler and he became friends. With Rudolf Kryzanovsky,

whose brother had occasionally shared his room, Mahler prepared and published a piano-duet version of the work.

Throughout his life, Mahler's attitude to Bruckner's music oscillated between veneration and rejection; but it was never simply one of affection for a hopelessly impractical senior whose naïvety appealed to his protective instincts. The title page of Bruckner's *Te Deum* describes the work: 'For chorus, soloists and orchestra'. Mahler crossed these words out in his copy, replacing them with a description of his own:

For the tongues of heaven-blessed angels, for chastened hearts and for souls purified by fire.

He conducted Bruckner's symphonies whenever he could, doing much to establish their eventual popularity in Germany and Austria. When, after several years of publication, Universal Edition was about to reach the position from which it would begin to pay a royalty on sales of Mahler's own scores, he asked that the royalty be withheld to help finance Universal's

A photograph taken of Brahms at the end of his life. By this time he regarded the young conductor Mahler as a protégé

edition of Bruckner's symphonies; another fifteen years passed and Mahler was dead before any royalty was received on his works.

In fact it seems as though Mahler's view of Bruckner was coloured almost from day to day by his own musical preoccupations—as Alma Mahler put it, 'he reserved for himself the privilege of inconsequence': and his attitude to the work of other composers was equally changeable. Coupling Bruckner's name with that of Brahms he told his wife in 1904 that they were both 'an odd pair of second raters'. On another occasion he complained about Brahms's 'utterly barren music-making'; and once said that he was 'a puny dwarf with a weak chest', and one breath from Wagner's lungs would blow him away. Yet Bruno Walter bore witness to Mahler's admiration for Brahms's *Variations on a theme of Haydn*, and Alma Mahler to the pleasure he took in playing Brahms's chamber music.

Natalie Bauer-Lechner remembered a conversation with Mahler about the music of Liszt, in which he explained that, unlike Richard Strauss, he would never modify his dislike of Liszt's music, which to him was simply hack work. But after a performance of Liszt's *St Elizabeth* he declared the work to be 'the most wonderful atmospheric composition music it is possible to imagine'.

Mahler did not simply grow out of some works and into others. The oscillation of his opinions continued throughout his life: his financial sacrifice on Bruckner's behalf was made less than a year before his death, long after he had first decided that Bruckner did not matter. His rejection of Hugo Wolf's songs is often quoted; he remarked to the conductor Oskar Fried in 1910:

Of Wolf's one thousand songs I know only three hundred and forty-four. Those three hundred and forty-four I dislike.

This is likely to have been no more final than Mahler's other musical judgements; like many composers, he seems to have valued the music of others for the immediate creative stimulus it offered or refused him.

The student years and those which immediately followed them were prolific in ideas that were taken up and discarded. In 1877 he set to work on an opera, *Ernst von Schwaben*, based on a play by Uhland. A second opera on the fairy tale *Rübezahl* was in his mind between 1879 and 1883, and intermittently for several years afterwards. But between 1878 and 1880 he wrote the words and music of *Das klagende Lied*: 'This,' he wrote in 1906, 'was the first work in which I found myself as "Mahler" . . . I call it my *opus 1*.'

Das klagende Lied was written with great confidence and panache to secure his future by winning the Beethoven Prize, the annual award made by the Conservatoire for the best work submitted by a past or present student. Mahler explained to Natalie Bauer-Lechner that had his work satisfied the jury, which, he said included Brahms, the anti-Wagnerian critic Hanslick, Goldmark and Hans Richter the conductor, 'My whole life would have been different . . . I should not have had to go to Laibach and would have escaped my whole cursed operatic career'.

Donald Mitchell's analysis of the course of events, however, in his *Mahler, The Early Years*, suggests that on this occasion Mahler's resentments got the better of his intelligence and memory. He apparently found it necessary to prove to himself that his career had been blocked by a reactionary, malicious establishment. The jury included neither Hanslick nor Goldmark; it met in December 1880, only a month after Mahler had finished his score, so that it is very unlikely that he could have had copies ready to show; and in any case the jurors decided that no composition entered that year had reached the required standard. If, as is more likely, *Das klagende Lied* was submitted in 1881, its failure to win the prize in no way forced him into a conductor's post, for he had taken up his duties at Laibach before the jury even met.

When he did leave Vienna to become a conductor, Mahler the piano virtuoso, whose friends thought him capable of great triumphs, retired from the scene. For the future, piano playing was to be a private refreshment; his various working rooms always included a piano among the furniture, but very little music except Beethoven's Sonatas and the *Well Tempered Clavier* of Bach. Another Mahler was still to make his presence felt. He was to be known before long as a sharp, stinging wit whose aphorisms and epigrams were eagerly collected by journalists and preserved with gratitude by those who were not their intended recipients. The wit was to emerge later, for the young Mahler was a personality of almost startling earnestness.

Mahler triumphing over his predecessor, Wilhelm Jahn, as Director of the Imperial Opera in Vienna. The press is burning incense in Mahler's honour while Jahn holds resolutely on to his pension rights

Chapter 3

The Man

Mahler's life-story could be told in photographs. The ugly, anxious little boy grows into a handsome, refined, sensitive young man with a formidable beard to hide his immaturity. The young dictator of the orchestra at Cassel wears only a small moustache and looks intimidatingly Prussian. The conductor of the Hamburg Opera shows a face that has grown more firm while retaining its sensitivity and refinement, but the Director of the Imperial Opera in Vienna is clearly a fighter, whose face seems to express will-power and a sardonic habit of mind. While he was at Vienna a court official gently suggested that the best way to deal with an obstacle was not to run one's head into it. 'When I bang my head into a wall,' Mahler replied, 'it's the wall that gives way.' But the conductor in America grows into gentleness; it is possible to see a certain calm radiance in his expression; as death approaches, the face becomes again like the face of the sorrowful little boy.

The adult Mahler was a ready source of epigrams and aphorisms, and his wit was always a weapon. He took little delight in the ridiculous, and his words always had a sting. When his wife asked him why he always bought expensive clothes and shoes, he explained, 'Spitting on the floor won't make a Beethoven of you.' 'The rough edges of a man's personality, which he tries to smooth down, are usually the best part of him,' he said. Walter tells the story of the 'influential person' who 'recommended a new opera, saying that the composer, though of no particular standing, had, this time, produced something really lovely. Politely Mahler replied, "Nothing is impossible, but it's improbable for a horse chestnut to produce an orange." '

Mahler always had the knack of neat, epigrammatic expression: 'An artist shoots in the dark, not knowing where he hits or what he hits.' 'What people call "tradition" is slovenliness.' 'Ugliness is an insult to God.' He got a reputation for his bon mots. Bruno Walter recalled how a Viennese 'journalist who did a Sunday gossip column was perpetually bothering me for characteristic comments and actions of his at rehearsal'.

He told me (Walter continued) that he inclined instinctively to state things in this drastic manner, and experience had taught him that it was the quickest and surest way of making himself understood. With a grin he added that this practical result was more to his purpose than the complete accuracy of expression inevitably sacrificed for a neat 'mot'.

Walter found that Mahler could be both 'outgiving, sympathetic and helpful' but also capable of a quite staggering lack of considertion. To end a conversation which bored him when he was stopped in the street by a chance acquaintance, he ran across the road and caught the nearest tram-car, not pausing to make excuses or good-byes. On his walks about Vienna, street urchins would call out to him that he had lost his hat and he would start looking around for it before he realized he was actually holding it in his hand. After a meal on the open-air terrace of a restaurant one evening he wanted to wash his hands; without thinking he took the water jug from the table, went to the edge of the terrace and poured the water over his hands—and also over a group of diners on the lower terrace. Later in the same meal he did precisely the same thing. Often as not he was so preoccupied by his thoughts that he could not even decide what to order from a menu. He solved this problem simply by standing up, looking around for someone who was obviously enjoying his meal and then pointing him out to the waiter and ordering the same dish. A visit to the dentist once afforded an even more absurd instance of forgetfulness. Alma, who had gone with him, was sitting in the waiting room when her husband appeared at the door to the surgery and demanded which

The changing faces of Mahler. Centre: 1871—eleven years old. Top left: 1878—eighteen years old. Top right: 1883—twenty-three years old. Bottom left: 1894—thirty-four years old. Bottom right: 1909—Forty-nine years old

of his teeth was aching. Yet nobody regarded Mahler as a comic eccentric. He was too formidable, too hard, for that.

As soon as he could afford to do so, as conductor of the Hamburg Opera, he found a country home for his summer holidays, and there, always among mountains and lakes, he composed. Mahler was a passionate lover of nature and was a pantheist to the extent that he saw nature as the only certain manifestation of a divine mind. He was incapable of cynicism; his conversion to Christianity in 1897 was not simply a means of ensuring his position at the Vienna Opera; he loved the drama, music and poetry of Catholic worship, but it seems that he did not so much embrace the Catholic faith as salute it as another manifestation of the beauty, mystery and awe in which he looked for his God.

Mountains, lakes, animals and birds all stimulated his creative spirit. While he was working on the Third Symphony, in his retreat at Steinbach am Attersee in the Salzkammergut, Mahler invited Bruno Walter to visit him. He collected his friend from the landing stage as the lakeside steamer pulled in, and watched Walter admiring the crags of the Höllengebirge high above them. 'You needn't pay any attention to them,' he said. 'I've composed them already.'

In the same way, he composed the bird song which surrounded the 'Composing house' in the grounds of the home which he built for himself on the edge of the Wörthersee, at Maiernigg in Carinthia. Throughout his summer holidays he must have worked with enormous speed and assurance, leaving the winter months for polishing, revision and scoring; he took his relaxation in long, tireless walks, or he rowed or swam, driving himself in his leisure as he did at work. High above the ordinary world of men and women he found a freer air, an exaltation for which he found a musical symbol in the cowbells of the Sixth and Seventh Symphonies, the last earthly sound to follow the climber into his lonely rapture.

In some of its moods, Mahler's nature music conveys the sense of a potentially devastating power. Behind these awe-inspiring or sometimes terrifying passages in, for example, the opening movement of the Third Symphony, lay disturbing, sometimes fearful, personal

Below: Toblach in the 1880s
Top right: Mahler's composing house at Maiernigg
Below right: The 'Composing House' (Schnusputzelhaüschen) at Steinbach am Attersee

experiences. Alma Mahler described how sometimes he would race back to her from the 'Composing house' staring-eyed, white and speechless with terror. Even as an adolescent he was aware of other moods, expressed in some of his letters, in which he anticipated the heartbreak of *Das Lied von der Erde* and thought of Earth as the consoling mother who would take him to her breast and give him peace. But that was only one of the aspects of nature of which he was passionately aware. He looked at nature with awe, with love and with dread—for strength at least as often as for comfort.

Though he described his education as worthless, he was an avid and receptive reader who began his day not with the newspapers but with Goethe or the philosophers. He had read Kant, Spinoza and Schopenhauer as a boy and returned to them again and again; Nietzsche was another infallible stimulus. Walter noted his delight in *Don Quixote* and Natalie Bauer-Lechner his enthusiasm for Dostoevsky: both discovered his eagerness to read aloud whatever was pleasing him.

Jean-Paul Richter, the idol of the early romantics, was another favourite, as was E. T. A. Hoffman, the composer novelist whose grotesque fantasies seem to be Mahlerian in their imaginativeness.

The idea of 'light reading' was entirely alien to him. He read seriously, for stimulation and

mental sustenance rather than for information. Goethe and Nietzsche were the poets to whom he turned most frequently, though Rückert provided words for two sets of mature songs of great beauty. As a married man, he developed the habit of relaxing after lunch while his wife read to him:

It might be *Zwei Menschen*, by Dehmel, *Parsifal*, by Wolfram von Eschenbach, *Tristan*, by Gottfried von Strassburg, or a scientific or historical book. I went to a course of lectures by Professor Siegel at the University: *Astronomy from Aristotle to Kant*. I took notes on them and read them out to Mahler in the evenings. . . . In this way we came to Giordano Bruno and Galileo.

There is no trace of sarcasm in Alma Mahler's comment, 'He was touching in his eagerness to explain anything that I did not understand.' But even Alma felt that there was something misguided when, just before the arrival of their second child, Mahler set himself to calm her nerves while waiting for the midwife by reading Kant to her. On his deathbed he read Eduard von Hartmann's *The Philosophy of life*, tearing out the pages to do so because he was not strong enough to hold up the entire volume.

Himself an inveterate minor poet, his models were not the writers whose poetry he read most enthusiastically but the minor romantics of an earlier generation who inspired him to entirely conventional though carefully handled stanza forms: he bobs along quite smoothly in the wake of the romantics. More valuable as an indication of his mind is the poem he wrote for *Das klagende Lied*. The story is his own variant of a rather grisly folk tale, and the poem is close to the ballad style familiar to Germans of his generation through the ballads of Carl Loewe. The poems he wrote to his first love, Jehanne Richter, four of which became the *Lieder eines fahrenden Gesellen* are for the most part closer to the folk poetry of the famous anthology by Arnim and Brentano, which later was to provide him with material for songs of startling imaginativeness and originality. The first of the *Lieder eines fahrenden Gesellen* is an expansion of a poem in the anthology. It was not until later, in the *Kindertotenlieder* and the five Rückert songs, that Mahler found musical stimulation in more sophisticated poems.

He also read widely in science and was friendly with many scientists. Naturally, his interest was in the stimulus his creative mind received from scientific ideas, and he read always in the hope of finding some reconciliation in science between observable fact and his own tendency to mysticism, his search for knowledge of the Divine Mind in which he believed, and his hopes of immortality. These preoccupations overflow from time to time into his letters. Letter after letter begins with an explanation that he is writing in great haste and then runs on for a thousand or more words; other lengthy and detailed letters often end with the phrase 'in all haste'.

Yet despite this apparent impracticality, Mahler was entirely business like and efficient in everything that concerned his profession. The letters in which he advises conductors preparing performances of his works go straight to the serious problems and deal with them admirably, with lucidity and common sense. As the young Director of the Budapest Opera in 1888, he planned his budget and worked within it, organizing and administering the theatre to such effect that for the first time in its four years' existence it began to work at a profit. Later he survived ten years in the Directorship of the Vienna Opera despite controversy and campaigns against him, and the authorities in Vienna were very reluctant to lose him as Director. For he made the Opera there pay too and was as careful with the institution's money as he was careless with his own.

The poverty and the debts which dogged him until the last few years of his life were symptoms of the division in his mind between what pertained to music and what could be neglected because it did not. His sister, Justine, his housekeeper from 1889 until his marriage, was at least as impractical as he was. An apparently incurable financial situation was eventually brought under control only when Alma Mahler became his wife.

But no matter what money difficulties nagged him, Mahler was a generous man. When Bruno Walter, who had left Hamburg after two years for a more responsible post at Breslau, came to the end of his engagement there without a new post to go to, Mahler at once wrote offering him enough money to make it possible for him to live until another post came his way, without stopping to consider the hardship this would mean for himself. 'Luckily,' Walter wrote, 'I did not need to accept his sacrifice—for it would have been one; at the last moment I was offered an engagement at Pressburg.'

In 1910, Arnold Schoenberg had a similar experience of Mahler's generosity.

I am without money (he wrote to Mahler) and I have the rent to pay . . . I am compelled therefore to beg of you the loan of 300–400 krone. I shall certainly repay them next year when I am at the Conservatoire.

On the next day he wrote again to Mahler:

I have today received 800 krone in your name from Miethke. This is as speedy as goodness itself, which in a good man calls for no decision, and not even for any spur. It is the mere emanation of his being.

The rest of Schoenberg's letter is a remarkable outpouring from a man almost eager to resent the merest suspicion of patronage, distrustful of the motives of others. 'Can I thank you?' his letter continues,

I ought to be able to and I should like to. But it weighs heavily on me because I wish my veneration to have no extraneous source. Not that there is any danger; but I should like to honour you independent of gratitude.

'Veneration' was not the kind of term which Schoenberg bandied about freely. Mahler was likely to write with disarming friendliness to anyone who understood his music, but Schoenberg never found such freedom of response easy. His friendship with Mahler had begun in storms. As Director of the Vienna Opera, he represented an establishment which Schoenberg detested, and when they were brought together by Schoenberg's teacher, the composer Alexander von Zemlinsky, their first meetings seemed to end in vows of undying animosity— mutual attraction but a resolution not to yield to each other. Schoenberg saw Mahler's music, at

first, as the end of an outmoded style in which nothing new or valid could be done. In his collection of essays, *Style and Idea*, Schoenberg explained how he came to reverse his opinions after he had heard the Fifth Symphony; he remained from then on devoted not only to the personality of the older man but also to the music in which, he said, he found that personality completely expressed.

Mahler, for his part, saw something to respect in the younger composer. When Schoenberg's first String Quartet was howled down, in 1905, Mahler protested to one of the hissers: 'No need to get excited'. Rather unexpectedly the man replied, 'I hiss Mahler too'. Mahler struggled to gain a hearing from the *Chamber Symphony*, given an equally noisy reception in 1907. He said, after the performance, 'I don't understand his music, but he's young and perhaps he's right. I am old, and I dare say my ear is not sensitive enough'. Guido Adler, the musicologist, a friend of Mahler since they attended the Conservatoire together, telephoned Alma Mahler after the scenes at the Chamber Symphony performance begging her to stop Mahler endangering his precarious position in Vienna by supporting so scandalous a work.

Not even the young Walter, closer to Mahler than any other colleague or friend, was quite safe from Mahler's intransigence. Walter's

gentleness and simple friendliness, combined with his outstanding musical qualities, endeared him to Mahler when as an eighteen-year-old rehearsal pianist he came to Hamburg. Mahler encouraged him and set him off on an independent course. On taking up his appointment at Vienna Mahler gradually removed the old guard of Richter and his followers from the musical staff, and then he summoned Walter to Vienna to become his assistant. To his resentment and annoyance he found that his protégé was determined to remain independent until he felt mature enough to work closely with Mahler without being devoured by a more powerful personality. Mahler however, who was involved in one of his spells of violent over-work, felt that he had really asked a friend to share his musical burden and he had been let down. But when in 1900, Walter moved for a year to Berlin, the two revived their old relationship and a more mature and self-confident Walter rejoined Mahler in 1901 as second conductor in Vienna.

The oddest of Mahler's friendships was that with Richard Strauss. They met in 1885 when Strauss, four years younger than Mahler, was twenty-one. Strauss was impressed by Mahler's conducting and such of his composition as he saw at that time—his completion of Weber's unfinished opera *Die Drei Pintos*. Nine years later, Strauss moved heaven, earth and the German musical establishment, to have Mahler's First Symphony included in the Festival of the Allgemeiner Deutscher Musik-verein in Weimar in 1894. It was Strauss again who arranged for Mahler to conduct the Second Symphony in Berlin a year later.

'Strauss and I are two miners tunnelling from opposite sides of a mountain', said Mahler, adapting a phrase by Schopenhauer. 'One day we shall meet in the middle'. He refused to regard Strauss as a rival, though Strauss was a fine conductor and had made his reputation as a composer while still in his early twenties. He remained grateful for Strauss's support in his early days, and spoke of it always with gratitude. He admired some of Strauss's music enormously, and conducted several of his works. When, in 1905, the Viennese censorship refused, on religious and moral grounds, to sanction a performance of Strauss's *Salome*, which had made a sensation in Dresden at its first performance, he offered his resignation; he was doubly infuriated because the censors, rather than admit their action, maintained in public the pretence that the failure to produce the work was the responsibility of the Opera. However Mahler did produce Strauss's *Feuersnot* in Vienna, although that too was regarded as scandalous. He had a very high opinion of *Tod und Verklärung*, conducted the *Symphonia Domestica*, but disliked *Elektra* and was rather cool about many of Strauss's more popular orchestral works.

He also had other reservations about his great contemporary. Strauss was a careful business-man who thought it important that his works should make money; this attitude horrified Mahler. Neither could Mahler and his wife understand how a great composer could allow himself to be bullied by a shrewish ex-*prima donna* wife who preferred to discuss fashions rather than the weighty philosophical and aesthetic problems, who made scenes, and who was even ready to attack her husband's work in public. The idea that a great composer could enjoy himself playing cards as a relaxation was also quite beyond the Mahlers' comprehension.

The story of the friendship is told by Alma Mahler, never the most generous of commentators, and she makes it clear that neither her husband nor she could understand Strauss's often defensive facetiousness and his rare outbursts of anger. While the usually equable composer submitted gracefully to the demands of his wife, whom he adored, there were occasions when difficulties over rehearsal schedules or the importunities of local or national big-wigs drove him to unexpected fury: Strauss's intensity and sensitiveness were, as far as possible, kept out of sight, exactly controlled, so that the Mahlers thought of him not as an extremely sensitive creative mind, but as a musical tradesman given to pointless tantrums like a spoiled child. Mahler's rages, far more frequent and less controlled, were, according to Alma's account of things, the righteous anger of a frustrated prophet.

For his part, Strauss, who happily disguised himself as a down-to-earth Bavarian burgher, found it hard to understand why Mahler sold himself into slavery whenever he accepted a post. If he killed himself for the sake of the Vienna Opera, Strauss wanted to know, what good would it do? The almost neurotic seriousness of Mahler's way of life induced Strauss from time to time to attempt a cure through laughter. He admired Mahler with a generosity rare among composers who find themselves faced with a potential rival, and did all he could to win recognition for Mahler's work. The two miners, at the respective ends of their tunnel, both foresaw the inevitability of their eventual meeting in the mood of serene acceptance which marks the end of Mahler's Ninth Symphony and Strauss's *Four Last Songs*.

Everything Mahler achieved was won in spite of ill-health. In 1888, at the time of his departure from Leipzig, having done two men's work for over a year, and composed his First Symphony, his health gave way and he was put into hospital for an intestinal operation. From then onwards his health was never good. In 1901 a severe haemorrhage demanded surgical treatment and a long convalescence. The exhausting rehearsals which made angry orchestral players too weary to rebel, the feverish intensity of his working life and the energy with which he relaxed in long mountain walks were all part of a dangerous way of life for a man in precarious health.

In 1907 his doctors warned him that he had irreparably damaged his heart. It amounted to a virtual death sentence and he at once changed his way of life. He feared death and was conscious of the work he still had to do. He became inescapably conscious of his health, carried a pedometer in his pocket to be sure that he never walked too quickly, and rested every few hundred yards. The longing for death which he had expressed often enough since his adolescence evaporated as death approached. The slacker his hold on life became, the more passionately he loved it.

For the last ten years of his life, Mahler had to take account of the need to provide for a young wife and their children. His relationships with women, before his marriage, seem to have been among the almost comically incongruous aspects of the life created by his divided personality. In sexual matters he was puritanically inhibited. The flesh was to be beaten down so that the spirit would be set free from its claims, and though his youthful vegetarianism, which would redeem the human race by setting mankind free from the demands of physical appetite, did not last very long, he continued to regard any sort of physical indulgence as slavery to the flesh. Mahler's early love affairs came to nothing; sexual indulgence, of all indulgences, was the most enslaving. His sister Justine could barely summon up the

Anton Bruckner, who was Professor of Harmony at the Vienna Conservatoire during Mahler's student days. Mahler had some reservations about Bruckner's music, but did all he could to popularize it

courage to tell him that she and Alfred Rose, the great chamber music player and leader of the Vienna Philharmonic Orchestra, were in love and intended to marry; the idea of love had become so strange to him that Justine found it impossible to believe that he could understand their wishes or sympathize with their emotions.

His puritanism affected his professional dealings too. Sopranos and contraltos were called to his office to be rebuked for what he held to be their moral weaknesses. The offer of a casual love affair by a Hamburg soprano filled him with horror, and when Marie Gutheil-Schoder, who sang all three soprano roles in his Vienna production of *The Tales of Hoffmann*, appeared for the dress rehearsal of the Venice scene wearing a skirt slit up on both sides to her thighs, she was ordered off the stage by a furious maestro to have her 'indecent' dress sewn up into proper modesty.

For all that, in Cassel he fell in love with Jehanne Richter, a young soprano in the company, and the love affair provided the inspiration for the *Lieder eines fahrenden Gesellen*. The uncertainty of his future and, it may well be, an appetite for being in love which did not reach the point of desiring a firm relationship left him to enjoy the agony of loving in vain. In Leipzig, a love affair with the wife of Captain von Weber, the grandson of the composer, plunged him into a more dangerous situation. The lady, older than he, was not, it seems, fully prepared for a poetical experience of love denied by fate. They planned to run away together, but she missed the train, apparently to Mahler's relief.

His relationship with the twenty-three-year-old Anna Bahr-Mildenburg, who joined the Hamburg company in 1895, was more real. Under Mahler's tuition, she became a great dramatic soprano and the most devoted of his disciples. According to the Viennese critic Ludwig Karpath, who knew both Bahr-Mildenburg and Mahler well, the two actually became engaged in Hamburg. When Mahler left to take up his Directorship in Vienna he wrote her a series of letters which, while not passionate love letters, were the most intimate he wrote to any woman other than his wife. Within a year of Mahler's arrival at Vienna, Anna had joined the company there.

The fact that Mahler and she were together in Vienna on terms of close friendship for three years before his marriage to Alma, suggests that neither Mahler nor his most devoted disciple can have been specially eager to marry. Alma, who gives a very ungenerous account of Bahr-Mildenburg's attempts to restore whatever intimacy had existed between her and the conductor in the past, never mentions the engagement between them, but explains that Mahler himself told her that his relationship to the great soprano had never been more than an affectionate comradeship-in-arms. Karpath is the only one of Mahler's friends to have mentioned the engagement, but though Bahr-Mildenburg, who lived until 1947, hotly contested several points in his book, she never contradicted the story of her engagement to Mahler.

Alma Maria Schindler, whom Mahler met and fell in love with in 1901, was the daughter of one distinguished painter, Anton Schindler, and step-daughter of another, Carl Moll. She was twenty-three, had grown up in enlightened, comfortable surroundings and was a talented pianist. She was, too a composer of some promise. Their friends, seeing a dangerous similarity in their temperaments, tried to dissuade them from marriage. Carl Moll warned his step-daughter against taking Mahler too seriously because he was generally known to be deeply in debt and his position at the Opera was insecure. But while Mahler hesitated, Alma was determined.

Mahler's hesitation was partly understandable, in that he questioned the wisdom of marrying a girl so much his junior, and partly neurotic—he seems to have doubted his right to marriage and happiness. Alma's account of their courtship faces their difficulties honestly, though it says nothing of what she herself hoped for from marriage to a difficult, middle-aged celebrity. She understood his hesitations but was in love with this lovable, in many ways ingenuous, man. She felt it to have been her mission in life to love, support and guide a great artist, and Mahler was by far the greatest artist she had met. To overcome his doubts and to make their marriage inevitable, she slept with him and became pregnant.

But Mahler never asked for support and was as susceptible to guidance as a runaway railway train; the only route he could follow was that which he had already decided for himself. Alma could never make herself the moral and spiritual driving force behind his work, and therefore she became unhappy, feeling that he had excluded

A painting of Richard Wagner by Lenbach. Mahler disregarded Wagner's anti-semitism, adored his music and based all his work in the opera house on Wagner's principles

her from his real life. She was, she came to believe, no more than a habit to which he had grown accustomed; he took life from her and gave her nothing in return. His treatment of her compositions seemed to her symptomatic of his attitude; before their marriage he had worked with her enthusiastically, suggesting improvements; after the marriage they ceased to exist for him, though he trusted her critical insight, assumed her absorbed interest in everything he wrote and exploited her willingness to make fair copies of his work as it progressed. He had the egocentricity of the creative artist, to whom nothing but his own work is quite real. Alma quotes a passage from the diary of Ida Dehmel, wife of the Poet Richard Dehmel, which analyzes the Mahler–Alma situation. It ends: 'He behaves as if he were a delicate instrument to be fenced round by the barbed wire entanglement of egoism'.

But Mahler's letters, whenever he was away from Alma, are full of longing for her and sorrow at their separation, even if it lasted only a day or two; people who knew them never doubted his adoration of his young, beautiful wife. Her unhappiness was primarily caused by the frustration of her desire to be the dominating force over a great creative mind, and Mahler was born to dominance, not to domination.

Nevertheless, he took it for granted that her efficiency and sense of order would make sense of his tangled finances. To do this she allowed herself to be shut out of any social life they might have shared. She refused invitations even to official functions because she would not buy new clothes until she had paid off his debts. For the first time Mahler was comfortably off, and he took it all for granted.

Alma helped to foster his friendship with younger musicians, like Schoenberg and Alexander von Zemlinsky, who became his most devoted admirers and redoubtable fighters of his battles. Through her and her step-father (who, like her mother, became his devoted friends) he came to know Vienna's leading painters and sculptors, so that his interest in the visual arts increased, making it possible for him to complete his work at the Vienna Opera by revolutionizing ideas of stage design and decor. But at the same time, she froze out of his life older friends whom she believed to be unworthy of him; not only Bahr-Mildenburg but the devoted and apparently undemanding Natalie Bauer-Lechner, the poet Siegfried Lipiner and the musicologist Guido Adler had little contact with him after 1902. She was as jealous as Gustav in her determination to keep for herself as much of him as he could give.

Their first child, Maria Anna, was born in November 1902, and their second Anna Justina, in June 1904. The elder, Mahler's favourite, died of scarlet fever in 1907, the year when his career in Vienna ended in storms and he learnt that his heart was incurably affected; it was, too, the year when Alma's health broke down. It became her duty to recover and look after a husband who immediately became obsessed by his own failing health, but the distance between the two was not lessened by affliction. In 1910, their marriage seemed to be falling into ruins because the architect, Walter Gropius (whom Alma married after Mahler's death and a stormy love affair with the painter Kokoschka), made Alma for a time believe that he could give her the fulfilment and happiness she needed; Mahler went to Sigmund Freud for advice. Freud, who had known Alma's father, pointed out that in marrying another artist much older than herself, Alma had attempted to replace the father she idolized. Conversely, he suggested that Mahler looked to his wife to replace his adored, suffering mother. The tragedy of their marriage, Freud explained, was that neither Alma nor her husband could play the role in the other's life that each desired to fill.

Nothing in Mahler's life outside his music is as great as the way in which he worked to rebuild his marriage. In spite of affliction, he converted himself to a realization that Alma was a person, not merely an appendage of his own will. At last he came to accept her as his equal, as an ally, lovable for her own qualities. Her songs were brought out and, without his help but to his delight, heard at a recital in Vienna. The new gentleness that appears in the later photographs belongs, one can believe, to the new relationship he achieved with her. Struggling to accept the inevitability of death, he worked on the unfinished Tenth Symphony revealing a new fine-drawn, prophetic style which makes it tragically plain how much further he was still able to travel in new musical territories. Yet the notes, jottings, doodles and exclamations which are to be found on so many of his sketches turn out, on the sketches of the Tenth, to be messages to Alma, uttered with a devotion, a sense of dependence and love, which he found only at the end of his life.

Right: Alma and Gustav with their daughter Anna on a family outing with friends in 1910
Below: Mahler and Anna Bahr-Mildenburg walking in the Vienna woods; rumour declared that they were engaged to be married

Chapter 4

The Road to Vienna

Mahler's letters and reported conversations return almost obsessively to the harshness of the fate which made him a conductor. His life in the theatre was hell. To prepare a work for performance was a painful martyrdom. He had been condemned, by poverty and the failure of his compositions to earn a living, to a life of galley slavery. He would, he often explained, have preferred any life to that of a conductor.

For Mahler, conducting was a war on two fronts—with the musical notation which sometimes hid the secrets it is meant to reveal, and with the musicians he conducted, who could not share his unbridled fanaticism. Their inability to achieve almost unheard of refinements of nuance, phrasing and *rubato* was, to him, nothing but a bovine refusal to spend themselves as completely as he set out to spend himself in the service of music.

Late in life he seems to have begun to understand his strange relationship with his practical work more clearly. In a letter to Bruno Walter he said that when he was conducting, all his problems evaporated, and to Guido Adler he wrote:

I must have some practical outlet for my musical abilities to balance the great inner experiences of my creative work.

A conductor cannot be great and gain no satisfaction from his labours. It is impossible to believe that Mahler really hated conducting while he was actually working out subtle interpretative problems. He hated conducting because it forced him to cram the creative work, his divine mission, into his summer holidays; he hated it with almost frightening violence when it trapped him into responsibility for the type of routine performance which he believed to be a blasphemy against music. But it was necessary to him.

In many theatres, his attitude had some justification. Any opera taken into the repertory was revived year after year with little or no rehearsal. Performances became a routine and even serious, accomplished musicians came to believe that they could be nothing else. Stereotyped performances, once they became the standard, killed enthusiasm. It became natural for players to resent the angry little fanatic who suddenly imposed a punishing work load on them. Exhaustive sectional rehearsals of works that they knew off by heart were followed by full orchestral rehearsals before the final rehearsals with singers and chorus could begin. The coldly angry, sarcastic perfectionist on the podium would have infuriated the orchestra at Cassel (Mahler's first major appointment) even if he had been a conductor of vast experience; as he was a boy in his twenties, he became intolerable to them. Perversely, Mahler seems to have found satisfaction in realizing the intensity of their dislike.

Ruthlessness, a merciless, scathing tongue and complete tyranny over the players, made possible only by an unflawed will and an arrogant conviction of the rightness of his views were essential ingredients of Mahler's effectiveness as a conductor. The strange, tense relationship of conductor and players made for performances of extreme intensity and electric force. It is almost as though the anger and the resentment had to be aroused so that in defeating them, Mahler made the triumph of his will complete and imposed his interpretation of the music. Thus he brought the conflicts in his own personality out into the public arena and made them serve music. He regarded these battles and victories as a necessary part of his work; the rehearsal over, he was prepared to return at once to a state of normal courtesy.

Arriving in Rome once to conduct, he was told by Willem Mengelberg that the orchestra was poor and needed to be ruled with a firm hand. Mahler therefore mounted the podium and, before a note was played, using a dictionary, he launched into a violent denunciation of the laziness, stupidity and ignorance of the

Otto Boehler's silhouettes of Mahler conducting in Vienna. Later, his style as a conductor became extremely restrained

41

during the interval. He earned thirty gulden a month, with an additional fee of sixty kreuzer for every performance he conducted.

This was the bottom of the ladder. In the following year he became conductor at Laibach (Ljubljana), disguising his youth behind a considerable beard, but he did not see his future as tied up with this new art; it was simply a way of earning a living, and Laibach did nothing to arouse his enthusiasm for the work. He made no attempt to conduct Wagner and Mozart—he preferred to protect them from ill-usage; his greatest feat seems to have been to conduct Gounod's *Faust* with a single male voice in the chorus—its owner marching across the stage roaring the Soldiers' Chorus.

Laibach was in the lowest rank of German theatres, but by the time he left there for Olmütz (Olomuc), Mahler had developed the conducting technique which he eventually refined from extreme vigour of gesticulation to almost immobile simplicity. Olmütz was better than Laibach, but not good enough in Mahler's view for the classic German repertoire. He conducted Méhul's *Joseph in Egypt*, operas by Verdi and Meyerbeer, Flotow's *Martha* and, with considerable daring, Bizet's *Carmen*, only five years old and still very controversial. *Carmen* and *Martha* were responsible for his next step up the ladder. Treiber, *Kapellmeister* of the Royal Prussian Court Theatre in Cassel, went to see *Carmen* and stayed on for a performance of *Martha*, apparently impressed with the young conductor. When, a few weeks later, Treiber found himself left without a second conductor, he offered the post to Mahler, who accepted it and began his Cassel appointment in June, 1883.

There is no single point at which we can say that Mahler accepted his destiny as a conductor. Possibly the better work he had done at Olmütz awoke some ambition, for Walter and others noticed his love of Verdi's music and the care he took of its obvious, apparently simple orchestration; *Carmen* was a work he never ceased to love. Possibly the realization of his ability as a conductor of these works, together with the disregarded potentialities of the Cassel Opera, worked together to awaken his blazing fanaticism.

The legend of Mahler the great conductor begins at Cassel. The theatre was orderly, adequately staffed and capable of mounting performances of the Mozart and Wagner

players, who walked out of the rehearsal and later went through the concert in a spirit of passive disobedience. Walter, a fundamentally gentle man, tried to persuade Mahler to curb his ruthlessness and was surprised at the naïvety of his friend's reply. Mahler believed that his harshness had no lasting effect on those who suffered from it. 'Once the first unpleasantness is over,' he said, 'I'm immediately good again.' He convinced himself that his work with any orchestra was inevitably a battle. 'As a human being, I'm prepared to make every concession,' he declared. 'As an artist, I make none. Anybody who fears he might lose a battle has already lost it.' It was essential that he always won and the performance was a celebration of his victory.

The career which he hated but would not abandon came to him almost by accident. In 1880 he was a young composer earning what living he could as a piano teacher. Characteristically, he was prepared to endure poverty and obscurity until Julius Epstein suggested that he should apply for the conductorship of the Summer Theatre at Bad Hall, in Upper Austria. The theatre accommodated an audience of less than two hundred and presented only operettas and farces. Mahler did everything, distributing and collecting the orchestral parts, dusting the piano and, according to his account of the engagement to his wife, pushing the manager's baby round the theatre in her pram

Above: Mahler, the dictatorial, sarcastic assistant conductor of the Opera at Cassel
Below: The Court Theatre at Cassel, where Mahler had his first experience of work in a well-run theatre and where he declared war on operatic routine

operas, and of Beethoven's *Fidelio*, though these were the prerogative of the *Kapellmeister*. Singers and players alike, however, trudged their way through the repertory apparently unaware that repertory productions deteriorate and that only constant vigilance and frequent rehearsal can maintain standards. Mahler, regardless of his very limited official powers and minor position, set out single-handed to reform musical corruption and re-establish ideals. Soloists, chorus and orchestra found themselves not merely rehearsing operas which they had performed over and over again to general satisfaction. They were faced with exhaustive sectional rehearsals. A small, pale tyrant with blazing eyes and a merciless tongue gave them no quarter. Mahler won a following in the audience, for he created a tension and an excitement new to Cassel. Chorus and orchestra loathed him.

Once a friend warned him to miss a chorus rehearsal he had called; the men were coming armed with sticks to beat him up. Instead of avoiding danger, punctual to the moment Mahler strode into the rehearsal room and plunged at once into unusually strenuous work; he prolonged it until he had achieved everything he wanted and then, with a long, contemptuous look at his underlings, he strode out unharmed.

Mahler failed to convert Treiber—'The best four-in-a-bar conductor I've come across,' he wrote to Friedrich Lohr—of the necessity of reforming his own ways, so that Treiber found himself treated with as little consideration as the orchestra and chorus. Months before his two-year contract came up for reconsideration, Mahler was looking for an escape. He wrote to Hans von Bülow, a conductor he admired, asking to be accepted as a pupil and assistant. Bülow did not answer his letter but simply sent it to the Cassel management. So Mahler opened negotiations with Leipzig Municipal Theatre.

Nothing was decided when, in June 1885, Mahler's admirers appointed him conductor of a three-day festival, the programmes of which would include Mendelssohn's *St Paul* and Beethoven's Ninth Symphony. It was not in his nature to refuse an opportunity to conduct the symphony which is perhaps the greatest challenge and the highest potential satisfaction of a conductor's career and the idea that to accept the invitation might be tactless meant nothing to him. He described the course of events to Friedrich Löhr:

The Orchestra is on strike because this makes the *Kapellmeister* look ridiculous. The General-intendant has had the cheek to appeal to my better nature and ask me to give up the Festival. Naturally, I said what I thought, so now I'm a dead man as far as the theatre is concerned.

The Festival was a great success. Grateful patrons presented Mahler with a laurel crown, a gold watch, and a diamond ring; the *Casseler Tageblatt* described him as a '*Talentvoller Musiker* of great spirit and energy'. But the day of his glory was the day on which his contract was to be reconsidered—it was not renewed. Characteristically, Mahler saw himself as a blameless martyr to high musical principles hindered by the spiritless complacency of Treiber and the Opera management, who had not only refused to join him in his policy of reformation but had expected him to betray the cause of music by surrendering the Festival to lesser men. Not unnaturally, the management saw things otherwise.

This young man, who gave rise to high hopes when he arrived, has lost all interest in his work and has continuously to be reprimanded, because of his hopes of an engagement in Leipzig. He should shine as a Festival conductor, but here he had lost the confidence of the choir as well as the orchestra.

His Leipzig engagement was for the season 1886–7. To fill the gap of several months before he took up his new duties, he went as second conductor to the notable Wagner conductor Anton Seidel, at the Deutsches Landestheater in Prague. The Director of the theatre was Angelo Neumann, who had planned the first production of *Der Ring des Nibelungen* outside Bayreuth. His devotion to Wagner had not been acceptable to Cosima Wagner, the composer's widow, because Neumann was not convinced that the productions supervised by Wagner were the last word on Wagnerian decor and style of production. Mahler, whose ideas of Wagnerian *tempi* were more varied and extreme than those of Bayreuth, was a conductor Neumann was determined to encourage. The young conductor at last got his hands on *Lohengrin, Das Rheingold* and *Die Walküre*, as well as on Wagner's edition of Gluck's *Iphigenia in Aulis* and Beethoven's *Fidelio*. Had Neumann succeeded in keeping Mahler with him, he might have trained the conductor in humanity, for he discovered Mahler's determined intransigence and managed to mitigate its effects without infuriating the fanatical young man.

When he took up his duties at Leipzig Mahler found his new post a disappointment after the freedom of Prague. He had refused to accept the engagement until he was promised the right of sharing the Wagnerian repertory with his superior, the great Arthur Nikisch, but it was not very long before he discovered that the promise made by the Opera Director, Staegemann, was worthless because Nikisch had no intention of sharing anything he wanted to monopolize. Nikisch was a superb conductor, with a remarkable expressive technique, though Mahler said that the ultimate heights and depths were beyond him; half of him was a dedicated musician, but the other half had the insatiable vanity of the traditional *prima donna*. He was so efficient, according to Mahler, that sometimes the young man felt that he might himself have been conducting.

But before long Mahler was thinking of a move. After he had been only three months in Leipzig he wrote to Friedrich Löhr outlining his prospects. He was quite confident that the Leipzig contract would be renewed; Pollini, the manager of the Hamburg *Stadtsoper*, had offered him an engagement; he could go to Karlsruhe as *Kapellmeister*; Neumann had made him a splendid offer. 'The donkey is standing between four bundles of hay. Which one should I have?'

In the event, he refused them all. Nikisch fell seriously ill, and for five months at the beginning of 1887 Mahler was in sole musical charge of the Leipzig Theatre. When the period of strain and over-work ended and he plunged into almost feverish work on the First Symphony, Staegemann, who had come to regard him as a hero ready to give his life to the Leipzig Opera, found official duties taking second place to the claims of composition. By the time the Symphony was completed, Mahler's health was in ruins and Staegemann disappointed in his conductor. He complained to Mahler, who promptly resigned—though none of the posts open to him at the end of 1886 were available—and his resignation was accepted.

By this time, it is possible to see that Mahler was a fanatical perfectionist whose determination to achieve the highest standards took absolutely no account of his own or anyone else's feelings. The first glimpse of his quality, apart from the untrustworthy guidance of public acclamation, comes from Richard Strauss

Right: A model of the Royal Opera House, Covent Garden, as it was in 1892, when Mahler conducted a season of German Opera there
Overleaf: This painting of the Vienna State Opera House is by Oscar Kokoschka, a contemporary of Mahler

Left: The Deutsches Landestheater in Prague. In 1885 Mahler conducted operas by Wagner here for the first time

Top: Cosima Wagner, more virulently anti-semitic than her husband, intrigued against Mahler because of his Jewish birth and, despite his reputation as a Wagner conductor, refused to invite him to Bayreuth Above: Arthur Nikisch, conductor of the Gewandhaus Orchestra in Leipzig from 1879–89. He already had a great international reputation before Mahler became his assistant in 1886

Left: The Metropolitan Opera House, New York, where Mahler conducted for the first time in 1908

in 1887. The young Bavarian conductor-composer wrote to his mentor Hans von Bülow in November 1887:

I have made a very attractive new acquaintance, Herr Mahler, who appears to me to be a highly intelligent musician and conductor; he is one of the few modern conductors who understands *tempo* modification, and he expressed splendid ideas generally, particularly about Wagner's *tempi* (opposed to those of the accepted Wagner conductors of today).

Mahler's next post was even more eloquent testimony than Strauss's admiration to the quality of his conducting. In the summer of 1888, Franz von Benickzy, Intendent of the Royal Court Theatre in Budapest, engaged him as Musical Director of the Theatre, with a contract for ten years and an annual salary of 10,000 florins. Though only twenty-eight, he was now the chief musical authority of an important theatre; he could prove his ability as an administrator and set standards of production that matched his perfectionist ideals. The theatre had been set up in 1884 as the first step towards creating a national Hungarian style of opera; but such limited popularity as it had won rested on the standard Italian and German operas. These were sung with international stars in the leading roles and often in multilingual versions, each of the celebrities of the cast singing his role in the language in which he had learnt it.

Typically, Mahler went to Budapest optimistically ready to create a national opera in a language he could not speak. In his letter to the company on taking up his appointment, he dedicated himself to the task of making the Opera House 'the focal point of all Hungarian artistic ambitions'. 'Teamwork' was to be the company's motto, and he promised to set 'an example of hard work and honest dealing'.

The great stars disappeared as, in two and a half years, Mahler built a resident company capable of answering all his demands. In January, 1891, Brahms went reluctantly to a production of *Don Giovanni*, expecting a conventionally tame, typically nineteenth-century performance. He found himself instead listening to a conductor who felt the greatness, the driving force and the dramatic passion of the opera; it was to turn him into a supporter of Mahler the conductor at a crucial moment in Mahler's career.

The Opera in Budapest began to make money as it filled with an audience which wanted the intensity and excitement which Mahler provided. Everything was controlled according to a budget which Mahler drew up with the utmost practicality and observed strictly. Because he believed that opera should be 'the focal point of artistic ambitions' and that audiences should experience opera as musical drama he arranged for the translation of libretti into Hungarian, supervizing the translation of Wagner's texts himself. But despite his success in setting a tottering theatre on its feet and the enthusiasm with which he had made use of political policies for artistic ends, extremists in the Nationalist party could not accept a Bohemian-Austrian-Jew with no true interest in Hungarian nationalism as a fitting leader for a Hungarian institution. When Benickzy resigned in February 1891, he was replaced by Count Zichy, an extremist who regarded Mahler as an interloper. To get rid of the foreigner, Zichy disregarded the terms of Mahler's contract and interfered in the artistic control of the theatre; Mahler fought back until, one day, he found himself locked out of his office in the theatre. He at once resigned, demanding compensation for the years of his contract which were still to run. He left Budapest with 25,000 florins in addition to his salary, in time to take up the post of conductor at the Hamburg Stadttheater in April, 1891.

This was a step down from the eminence he had occupied in Budapest; it gave him a free hand over matters of repertory and casting but left him without any control of matters of decor and production. His salary was 13,000 marks a year with a guaranteed 1,000 marks for an annual benefit performance. But at Hamburg he had a first-rate orchestra and company of singers already at his disposal; all he had to do was to turn a fine orchestra and company into lovers of his conception of music.

The manager of the Hamburg Opera, Pollini, had been born Bernhard Pohl but had adopted an Italian name whilst singing as a tenor in an Italian company which he had subsequently come to manage. A keen business man, his readiness to hurry exciting new works on to the Hamburg stage and his determination to enrol the best singers and musical staff, as well as good producers and designers, had made a fortune for him and given him control of the *Stadttheater* in Altona and the Thalia Theatre in Hamburg; the artists called him 'Monopollini'. As long as Mahler filled the theatre and kept the Opera in the news, Pollini was ready to allow him his head and to leave him in peace. Mahler stayed in Hamburg six years, increasingly irritated by what he regarded as the blatant commercialism of Pollini's policy and growing more and more depressed by the theatrical routine which determined that the 'show must go on,' even though the conductor might think it inadequate.

Mahler had worked out his *modus vivendi* between his two careers so that conducting and composition never came into conflict. Every opera he conducted was rehearsed to the point at which Mahler believed its musical presentation to be faithful to its composer's musical and dramatic ideals.

Bruno Walter, who went to Hamburg as chorus accompanist in 1894, soon found that Mahler knew scores by heart, and started with a clear picture of what he intended to achieve; the stage itself, the scenes and decor envisaged for the work, the singers and the unfolding dramatic situation all stimulated him towards solving the work's problems. The result was not simply a beautiful texture, convincing *tempi* and musical expressiveness, but music as drama, springing from the characters and situation occupying the stage. Walter remembered a performance of *Lohengrin* in Hamburg which was, for him, a musical revelation:

In the scene outside the cathedral, where Elsa and Ortrud are quarrelling, I suddenly realised the nature of opera. Mahler was not just conducting the accompaniment to a contralto song: he was with Ortrud in spirit; he was Ortrud; he was transporting both orchestra and singer into the mind of a deeply humiliated woman. At the same time, his music took in Elsa's terror and her profound belief in Lohengrin. His conducting penetrated to the soul of the music, and directly to its dramatic essence.

The demands Mahler made on singers were exceptional; he expected not only beauty of voice and clarity of diction but also both a sense of drama and an actor's ability to project a dramatic situation. In a conversation in 1901 he discussed the opera-singer's art, referring in particular to Anna Bahr-Mildenburg, who eventually followed him to Vienna, and to Marie Gutheil-Schoder, who reached the Vienna Opera shortly after his accession to power there and became a popular favourite.

You admire Madame Mildenburg as the greatest dramatic soprano of our day. She wasn't always like that. As a beginner she was clumsy, almost wooden. I taught her to watch every action she made, every gesture and every expression, in a mirror, as part of her musical training. To teach her to achieve a graceful carriage, I made her take walks without an umbrella, a muff or anything in her hands. I asked her to do physical exercises every night and morning.

He had, he said, been through every note and every nuance, every movement, gesture and expression of her roles with her, as he had been with Gutheil-Schoder, so that every part she played was projected with lively personality, emotional truth and apparent spontaneity.

Mahler applied no hard and fast technical rules but worked through what Walter called 'intuition and impulse'. Conscious of the effect he desired to achieve and the problems involved in achieving it, he set out to solve them as if they were new in every performance because they related in a special way to whatever body of musicians he was dealing with. He had little to say about conductors' technique or method. At first his own technique was home-made, extravagant, gesticulatory and energetic, and it is easier to understand his ideas from his criticism of others than from his random, infrequent explanations of his own principles. In 1898, he found himself talking about the failings of most of his contemporaries:

One can hardly believe how low the requirements of most conductors have become. Their chief eagerness is to get the beat right; phrasing is a complete mystery to them, and the idea of declamation gets lost in the process of time-beating. That is why they go so wrong over *tempi*, because it hasn't yet dawned on them that it is the *tempo* which brings a work to life, to creative fulfilment. It takes a mature, highly conscious human being, capable of thought and feeling, to solve the conductor's problems—one who can think and feel as the composer thought and felt when he created the work.

Because, 'the most important things about music are not in the notes', the conductor's greatest requirement is not technical expertise but the imaginative re-creative power to see the meaning and intention behind whatever appears on paper.

Mahler said little that can be taken away and used by other conductors for their guidance. What little he said concerns *tempi*. The Richter-Cosima Wagner school believed that he erred on the side of excessive speed, especi-

Above: Hans von Bülow, gouache by Lenbach

The Orchestra of the Budapest Royal Opera in 1889. Mahler, wearing a hat, is sitting in the second row, second from the right

The Stadttheater, Hamburg. Mahler was musical director here from 1891 to 1897, and it was during these years that he won his outstanding reputation

ally in his treatment of Wagner, though his performance of *The Mastersingers* was actually longer than Richter's. It was not excessive speed but a tendency to make all speeds, fast or slow, more extreme than the Bayreuth standard, which misled his opponents. His comments on performance always stress the paramount importance of clarity and distinctness. Alma Mahler noted some of his pronouncements:

The *tempo* is right if it allows every note its value. If a phrase can no longer be grasped because the notes run into one another, the *tempo* is too fast. The extreme limit of distinctness is the right *tempo* for a *presto*. Beyond that it has no effect. . . . If an *adagio* seems to be lost on an audience, he slowed the *tempo* down instead of quickening it, as was commonly done.

While Mahler's *tempi* were unconventionally extreme, he never allowed an orchestra to overwhelm the singers or obliterate the words; clarity was demanded for the text as well as for the music.

Indeed, distinctness and clarity were his obsessions; they lay at the foundations of his own style of orchestration, and its beauty is really an indirect result of his determination that the 'meaning' shall be clear. They explain his 'retouching' of the scores of Beethoven and Schumann. In 1892 Mahler conducted a brief German Season at Covent Garden, with a company largely of singers and players from Hamburg. Bernard Shaw, at that time the most eloquent and convinced Wagnerian in England, attended the performances as music critic of *The World* and noticed that the orchestra 'had a narrower graduation of tone from *pianissimo* to *fortissimo*' than the normal Covent Garden orchestra. Shaw noted the enthusiasm with which the audience accepted Mahler's conducting.

Walter, reporting long conversations with Mahler, noted his concern about *rubato*, the fractional stretching or compression of tempo for expressive effect, and his dislike of exaggerated tempo variations for the sake of expression or emphasis. His own performances employed *rubato* freely but with extreme subtlety and restraint, within narrow, precisely drawn limits; it was his need to control an almost infinitesimally fluctuating *tempo* which made necessary the intensive rehearsals which wore orchestral players into rebellion. Even in Italian operas, where he considered freedom of *rubato* essential, he strictly controlled it. As a result, his performances were alive from the first note to the last.

He was haunted by the fear of what he called 'subjectivity'. He noticed how powerfully it misled other conductors, who too often played a work in such a way that it lost touch with its composer's intentions and instead expressed

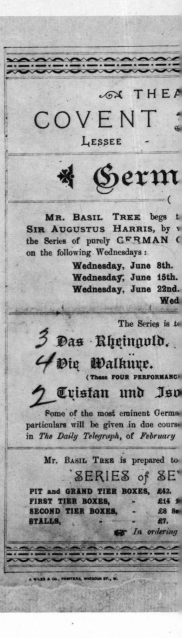

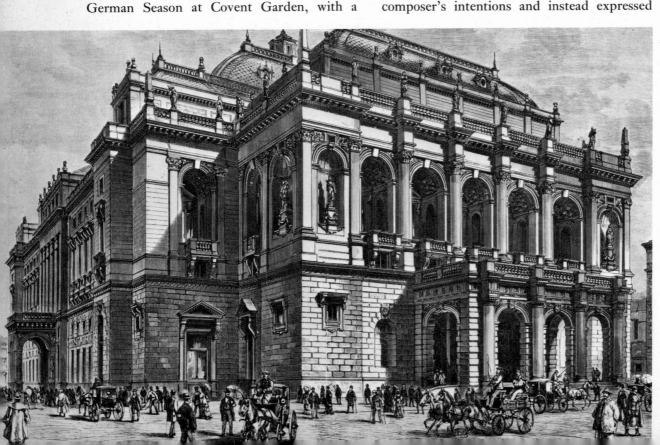

Left: The Royal Opera House, Budapest, where Mahler was Director from 1888 to 1891

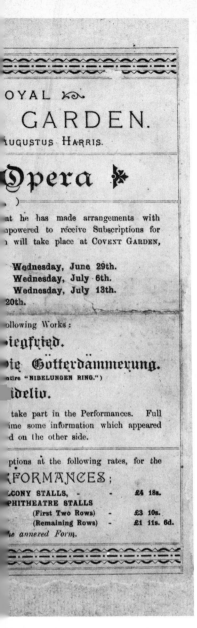

ROYAL &

GARDEN.

Augustus Harris.

Opera ❧

at he has made arrangements with
mpowered to receive Subscriptions for
n will take place at COVENT GARDEN,

Wednesday, June 29th.
Wednesday, July 6th.
Wednesday, July 13th.
20th.

ollowing Works:

Siegfried.

Die Götterdämmerung.

ntire "NIBELUNGEN RING.")

ideliv.

take part in the Performances. Full
ime some information which appeared
d on the other side.

ptions at the following rates, for the

RFORMANCES;

LCONY STALLS, - £4 18s.
PHITHEATRE STALLS
(First Two Rows) - £3 10s.
(Remaining Rows) - £1 11s. 6d.
e annexed Form.

Above: The announcement of the season of German Opera at the Royal Opera House, Covent Garden, in June, 1892. This was Mahler's only visit to London

the mind and feeling of the conductor, and he was determined to avoid this at all costs. Above all, Mahler strove to put himself into a composer's place and see the work in the score as the composer had first conceived it—to add his own thoughts and personality to it would be unforgivable.

Hans von Bülow, harshest and most unsparing of musicians in Mahler's early days, supplies proof that by the time he reached Hamburg, Mahler was a great conductor. He had not been there long when Bülow wrote to his daughter:

Hamburg now has a simply first-rate conductor in Herr Mahler who in my opinion is as good as the very best conductors. Recently I heard him conduct *Siegfried* . . . and I was filled with admiration when, without an orchestral rehearsal, he made that rabble whistle to his tune.

Bülow became quite uncharacteristically effusive to the young conductor, who regularly attended the concerts Bülow conducted in Hamburg. Their relationship was described in a letter from Mahler to Friedrich Löhr:

I go to all Bülow's concerts, and in his abstracted way he takes every opportunity of paying attention to me *coram publico*. He flirts with me (I always sit in the front row) whenever he reaches a particularly beautiful passage. He hands me the scores of unknown works down from his desk, so that I can follow them while the orchestra is playing. As soon as he sees me, he makes a deep bow; sometimes he talks to me from the podium.

Though Mahler the composer meant nothing to Bülow, Mahler the conductor became an honoured colleague. One day he sent a laurel wreath to the Hamburg Opera House, inscribed to 'The Pygmalion of the Hamburg Opera', indicating that as far as he was concerned, Mahler had brought that institution to life. Bülow was now sixty-two years old, worn out by work, nervous strain and the ravages of an unhappy temperament. The arrogant harshness which made him detested by many musicians and not a few audiences always spared his protégé Richard Strauss and Mahler, whom he treated as an equal. When his breaking health compelled him to abandon conducting, he asked Mahler to take over his commitments in Hamburg. Mahler took charge of the concerts for the season of 1894–5, after Bülow's death, and according to a letter from Mahler to his friend Arnold Berliner, the orchestra was not

entirely enthusiastic about the change:

A number of Marweges are sitting in front of me, I'm sorry to say, Herr Bignell being the chief of them; they are suffering for the purity of classical principles.

Marwege and Bignell were violinists in Bülow's Hamburg orchestra. They were among the musicians moved to indignation by Mahler's tendency to extreme *tempi* and unusual phrasings and nuances.

Mahler remained in Hamburg until 1897. In that time he had found assistants whom he could trust with operas from the standard repertory, except those of Mozart and Wagner, which he saved for himself. All the new works—they included Puccini's *La Villi* and *Manon Lescaut*, Humperdinck's *Hansel and Gretel*, Bizet's *Dajamileh*, Smetana's *The Bartered Bride* and *Dalibor*, Tchaikovsky's *Pique Dame*, Verdi's *Falstaff* and Rubinstein's *The Demon*—he conducted himself. After Bruno Walter's departure to Breslau and the resignation of the Second Conductor, Mahler found himself committed to conducting as many as four performances a week sometimes for periods of a month at a stretch; unless he could wholeheartedly approve of a subordinate's conducting, he would not delegate any duties to him.

His years in Hamburg had not been without trouble, for Mahler was born to trouble, and the need to work with a producer on the stage, the final authority of Pollini above him and the permanently strained relations with the orchestra were all fruitful sources of controversy. But his resignation, when it came, was the result of his dissatisfaction with repertory opera rather than of any major quarrel. The General Directorship of the Vienna Opera had become his goal because he believed only then, unhampered by stage directors and an intrusive, mercenary management, could he achieve his artistic aim—the complete integration of music and drama. Walter remembered, during his two Hamburg years, how often Mahler would joke about his forthcoming call to Vienna even before he had begun to work for it; every knock at the door was likely to be greeted by Mahler as his summons to go to the Vienna Opera and become 'The God of the Southern Regions'. Given the power to rule in Vienna, he could finally destroy the dead routine of repertory opera.

53

Chapter 5

God of the Southern Regions

Mahler had set his mind on the Directorship of the Vienna Opera, but not because he believed it to be a perfect organization. When he decided to leave Hamburg, he opened negotiations with Berlin, Munich and Dresden as well as Vienna, thinking that any of the four great court operas would have the resources and the prestige out of which he believed that he could mould a theatre perfect both dramatically and musically. Wherever he went there would be troubles, but the struggle would only convince him that he was on the right lines. Apart from Brahms, who supported him, the people who had most influence in Vienna, such as Hans Richter, first conductor at the Opera, and Hanslick, the leading Viennese critic, were to provide him with as much struggle as he needed.

He played himself in at the Opera in May, 1897, as *Kapellmeister* on trial for the Directorship. His performance of *Lohengrin*, though it had the barest minimum of rehearsals, immediately won the audience to his side; Wagner's most static opera came alive as a blazing dramatic experience. Mahler's immediate success led to his appointment as Director in the following October, when Otto Jahn, his predecessor, was unceremoniously hurried into retirement.

With Jahn as Director and Richter as First Conductor, musical standards at the Vienna Opera had been high. But they were not Mahlerian. Ill health had slackened Jahn's grasp on the institution by degrees and in any case, however good the standards, they were old fashioned; Richter, the conductor, had little time for any music since Wagner and new works had to wait a long time for production. Ever since Wagner had entrusted the first production of the *Ring* to him, Richter had enjoyed the trust of the composer's widow Cosima. She wanted to see Richter's reign continue in Vienna under the ailing Jahn because he staunchly cham-

pioned her husband's music and also because he had always tried faithfully to carry out his instructions to the letter. In fact, Wagner himself, towards the end of his life, seems to have come to the conclusion that Richter could only be trusted to interpret the operas correctly under his own personal supervision. Cosima also opposed Mahler's appointment on another ground—that he was a Jew.

But between them, Jahn and Richter had driven the Opera into a conventional rut. While the conductor could unfold a score with majestic conviction he was willing to sacrifice theatrical effect to the structure of the music; moreover his concentration on German music between Mozart and Wagner meant that the Opera had become totally unadventurous. The Intendant, or manager, von Bezecny, was determined on a change and Mahler the fiery modernist suited his book ideally. While he was a devoted Wagnerian he was also fascinated by such ungermanic works as *Carmen* and the operas of Verdi and could be relied upon to extend the Opera's repertory and at the same time to stimulate both the artists and the audiences. In the contract that von Bezecny drew up with Mahler, the new Director received the princely salary of 24,000 kroner and, more important still, was given almost complete power over the theatre and its staff. He had the support of the Emperor, Francis Joseph, though the Emperor seems at times to have laughed to himself at Mahler's determination to turn opera into a matter of almost religious solemnity. The Court Chamberlain, Prince Montenuovo—the Emperor's go-between with the management of the Opera—became an admirer and friend of Mahler until conservative criticism undermined his impregnable position. At first there was much in his favour and it was not simply through optimism that he wrote to Anna Bahr-Mildenburg:

Contemporary cartoon of Mahler introducing the 'wind of change' into the Opera

Everything is a fearful hubbub of congratulations, visits and so on. Thank God, the time of need is over! All Vienna has welcomed me enthusiastically. . . . There's no doubt I shall be appointed Director soon. . . . Everything is going famously! The entire personnel is on my side, and my position is outstanding, brilliant!

Mahler's ten years at the Vienna Opera can be divided into two acts. In Act One, he reformed the organization and its musical style. In Act Two he brought the stage presentation of opera into line with the company's musical achievements. Then a brief epilogue brought the swift fall which he could have prevented but fatalistically allowed to happen.

Before Jahn, conductors at the Vienna Opera had stood immediately in front of the footlights, thus depriving themselves of direct moment-by-moment control of the orchestra as they concentrated on the stage; Jahn conducted from a rostrum in the middle of the orchestra. Like him, Mahler sat to conduct opera, but he brought the rostrum to its modern position in front of the orchestra so that he was effectively in control of both orchestra and singers throughout every opera. Unlike that of La Scala, Milan, until Toscanini arrived there in 1898, the curtain of the Vienna Court Opera did not rise while the house lights blazed at full strength; lights were dimmed for the start of the music. Mahler, however, had them extinguished altogether before the music started. He was determined that the dramatic illusion should begin with the first note of the overture.

Mahler reorganized the method of rehearsal. He appointed a repetiteur to help him with rehearsals. But though he trusted him as much as he was ever able to trust a subordinate, he did not leave the preparation of an opera to the repetiteur until he himself was ready to take charge at orchestral rehearsals and undertake its final shaping and polish. He usually began work while soloists and chorus were still working on their parts with the piano. He put himself in charge of the learning of a work, rather than leave anything to chance.

He aimed to put the teachings of Wagner into practice. An opera was a *Gesamtkunstwerk* in which all the arts were united, each of them essential to the complete effectiveness of the composer's conception. Therefore Mahler himself acted as producer of many works from the Repertoire as well as of the new works which he introduced to Vienna. When events on the stage demanded his attention, he would leap from the rostrum and charge across the orchestra pit, scrambling on a double-bassist's stool to reach the stage. He not only controlled such directly musical features as the *tempo* and dynamics of an off-stage chorus or band in this way but, like Wagner himself, created groupings and suggested movements, gestures and facial expressions which stimulated singers towards their own interpretations.

The first intimation of the heart disease which was to kill him came to Walter and others of his

colleagues after one of these wild ascents of the stage; irritated by the wooden immobility of the chorus as Lohengrin's swan approached in Act One, Mahler rushed to pull them out of a straight line into some series of concerted movements which would express their excitement and astonishment. As he took the arms nearest to him and tugged them this way and that, a spasm of pain made him drop the arms and clutch his heart, but in a moment he was in action again.

Mahler, being the man he was, did not simply reform the musical system and its method of working; he set out to reform the audience as well. To the horror of easy-going Viennese music lovers to whom an evening at the opera was merely a pleasant relaxation, lateness was forbidden. Late-comers in the concert hall, still struggling towards their seats when the conductor was ready to start, were followed to their places by a malignant stare through the enormous spectacles which Mahler adopted to be sure that everything was within his field of vision. Late-comers to the opera were not allowed into the auditorium until the first act ended—a harsh prohibition if the opera were by Wagner and the first act an hour or more of continuous music. Mahler's edict prompted the Emperor to ask, 'Surely the theatre is a place one goes to for amusement?' It inspired a satirical journalist to suggest a system of signal cannons which would bring patrons from the farthest suburbs to the Opera in time to avoid traffic jams and be in their places when Mahler wanted them. Out-Mahlering Mahler, the satirist invented means of preventing gossip before the performance started and during intervals, prohibited the admission of unusually beautiful women who, by attracting too much attention, would destroy the dramatic illusion and of engaged couples likely to pay more attention to each other than to the performance; all couples entering together would have to prove their marital status before they were admitted.

Musical Vienna might find its new Director's notions quaintly eccentric, but the majority excused them for the sake of the dramatic power, intensity and splendour he gave them. For Mahler, they discovered, every performance was a Festival performance, rehearsed to hairline exactitude but alive in every note and presented with passion. In the event, most of the audience was prepared to accept his

tyranny; it was harder to deal with the singers' unofficial claques.

An official 'claque' of professional applauders provided with free seats so that it could demonstrate its approval, had always been accepted as a fact of operatic life. To ensure their personal success, singers were also in the habit of engaging unofficial claques paid to applaud all their most effective moments. When the first performance in Vienna of Smetana's *Dalibor* ended in open warfare between various groups of claqueurs, it was easy enough for Mahler to disband the official claque. Then Mahler demanded an undertaking from the singers never again to recruit claques of their own; reluctantly they agreed to do so, but the unofficial claques nevertheless continued. What could they do, the singers asked, to prevent the spontaneous approval of an audience moved by their singing?

Ironically, it was the pursuit of Wagnerian ideals which drove Richter, hitherto the high priest of Wagner, from the Vienna Opera. Until the arrival of Mahler the out-and-out purist, Vienna had tolerated cut versions of Wagner's operas. It had never, for example, seen the 'Norn' scene which is the prologue to *Götterdämmerung*. Mahler at once restored the cuts and announced that he himself would conduct all future Wagner performances. So far, he had gone out of his way to avoid any quarrel with Richter, but Wagner's one-time assistant naturally resigned in the face of public humiliation. Mahler was not sorry to lose a subordinate who disliked him and disapproved of his musical aims. He did not set out to rob Richter of glory or publicly to belittle him; he acted according to his conscience towards a great composer and was glad to see Richter go. With Franz Schalk, an ex-pupil of Bruckner, whom he almost trusted, and after 1901 Bruno Walter, in many respects his musical *alter ego*, as subordinates, Mahler could well spare the uncongenial Richter.

His success depended upon having a band of singers who would totally accept his doctrines. Not all the company he took over from Jahn was prepared to do this, and the audience was naturally grieved to see some of the old idols depart. Marie Renard, for example, beloved by Viennese audiences as a Carmen played 'as a woman to whom no drawing room would have been barred', stayed long enough to become a splendid Tatiana in Tchaikovsky's

The State Opera House, Vienna

Adèle
WIEN

I. GRABEN 19

*The 'Mahlersänger': Erik
Schmedes as Pagliacci (right);
Anna Bahr-Mildenburg as
Brünnhilde (left); Selma
Kurz the coloratura soprano
(far right); the young Leo
Slezak as Siegfried (below
right); Marie Gutheil-
Schoder as Carmen (below);
Leopold Demuth as Hans Sachs
(below far right)*

Eugene Onegin, one of the first novelties Mahler produced in Vienna, but she left the company to marry into the aristocracy after a farewell performance of *Carmen*, which, gaining intensity from Mahler's conducting, left the audience delirious with delight. Ernst van Dyck, a fine Lohengrin, and Franz Naval, Puccini's Rodolfo in the first Vienna performance of *La Bohème*, both left the Imperial Opera to make splendid international careers. In their place came Marie Gutheil-Schoder, whose Carmen was a violent, dirty, elemental gypsy, the Swedish tenor Erik Schmedes and, eventually, the gigantic, handsome Czech Leo Slezak, more perfectly equipped to look like the young Siegfried than any other Heldentenor in the history of opera.

If he could not have both a splendid voice and musical intelligence, Mahler preferred musical intelligence. Friedrich Weidmann, despite a voice generally described as 'hard', was a Hans Sachs whose vocal limitations were forgotten in the warmth and humanity of his acting. Selma Kurz, who joined the company as a mezzo-soprano, became a coloratura through Mahler's training, and was a moving Puccini heroine. Others arrived with limited reputations and became celebrities. Richard Mayr, from Salzburg, joined the company in 1902 after Mahler had heard him sing at Bayreuth; his voice was splendid, his care for an understanding of words exemplary; under Mahler he sang Verdi, Mozart, and Rocco in Beethoven's *Fidelio*; later, after Mahler's death, he was to impress his own personality and genius indelibly on the role of Baron Ochs, in Strauss's *Der Rosenkavalier*.

These, and others, were the *Mahlersänger*, a group so imbued with Mahler's spirit and dedication that it is tempting to describe them as an order rather than a company. They were stars of international luminosity who willingly gave their brilliance to Mahler's concept of ensemble opera. Singers who strove to serve the cause of opera were never Mahler's enemies; those who did not please him were abused, taunted and humiliated. For all that, when things went well, a rehearsal could be punctuated by Mahlerian witticism and carried on in high good humour. 'Don't keep looking at me so slavishly,' he said to one Siegfried. 'You mightn't like the result if you're staring at a conductor and sing straight into his face the line, "A horse it is, resting in deepest sleep".'

Despite Mahler, guest stars, especially the great Italian singers, had their own way in Vienna as they had everywhere else. Caruso sang at the Imperial Opera in 1906, just as he sang in all opera houses, determined that the production should fit him. Mahler seems not to have turned a hair when, in 1900, Dame Nellie Melba died movingly in *La Traviata* only to resurrect herself a few moments later and embark upon a virtuoso performance of the mad scene from *Lucia di Lammermoor*.

But the orchestra was rarely admitted to Mahler's good humour, partly because it never realized that off the platform he was a naïvely friendly man. At work, it had to fulfil its essential Mahlerian role as the enemy which had to be crushed. Yet when Franz Bartolomey, a clarinettist in the orchestra, lost a child during the rehearsals of Charpentier's Louise in 1903, he received a letter from the hated tyrant as from a friend grieving at his suffering:

I heard of your unhappiness only at the rehearsal, and I must thank you from the bottom of my heart that you made so great a sacrifice and attended the rehearsal in spite of your great sorrow. Please be assured of my gratitude for your determination to do your duty at such a moment, and accept my deepest sympathy with my warmest thanks.

To treat an orchestra with less than dictatorial authority, to admit its members as collaborators and to relax his hostility would, he seemed to believe, be an unforgivable compromise. The bitterness which had marked his work at Cassel and Hamburg continued in Vienna, where his Jewish birth seems to have exacerbated it. Though Mahler said that his race had never hindered his career, Alma Mahler told the story of two players from the orchestra. One, furious after a characteristically stormy rehearsal, was soothed by the other, who said, 'I don't know why you find Mahler so infuriating—Hans Richter pitches into us far worse.' 'Yes,' replied the angry one, 'He's one of ourselves. We can take it from him.'

When things went badly, Mahler did not scruple to pick out individual musicians, a procedure which always infuriates orchestral players. Worse still he had favourites. While Mahler did not stage-manage scenes of anger for the sake of gaining a musical effect, he did sometimes make an explosive situation pay musical dividends. Once he rehearsed the first four notes of Beethoven's Fifth Symphony—

'Fate knocking at the door'—over and over again until the orchestra was on the point of mutiny. 'Gentlemen,' he said, 'keep your fury for the performance, then at last we shall have the opening played as it should be.'

The orchestra seems to have recognized Mahler's greatness even if they found him intolerable in spite of it. The Viennese Philharmonic Orchestra—the Opera Orchestra in its role as a self-governing symphony orchestra—invited him to take charge of its concerts in 1898, and he did so for three stormy years. Yet in 1901, while he was on leave convalescing after protracted surgical treatment, the players took advantage of his absence to depose him and appoint a complete mediocrity, Josef Hellmesberger, ballet conductor of the Opera, in his place. Mahler's programmes during his three seasons were venturesome and original; they included Bruckner's Fifth and Sixth Symphonies, Dvořak's *Wild Dove* and *Hero's Song*, Strauss's *Aus Italien* and *Domestic* Symphony and his own *Lieder eines fahrenden Gesellen* and first two symphonies.

But the most unforgivable of all the humiliations Mahler imposed on his colleagues was suffered by Franz Schalk, even though Schalk was Mahler's own appointment. Obliged to hand over the conducting of *Lohengrin* to Schalk, Mahler called a special rehearsal to 'correct' Schalk's *tempi* although Schalk knew the opera well and had conducted it before he was called to Vienna. Mahler seated himself on a chair at the front of the stage and, baton in hand, conducted the unfortunate conductor, insisting that Schalk reproduce all the phrasing and nuances he was given as well as Mahler's *tempi*.

Apart from the novelties Mahler brought into the Philharmonic Concert programmes in Vienna, he expanded the repertoire of the opera. *Eugene Onegin* was produced in his first season; in 1898 came Bizet's *Djamileh* (of which Mahler had a very high opinion), Leoncavallo's *La Bohème* (originally more popular than Puccini's treatment of the same subject) and Reznicek's *Donna Diana*, remembered now only for its tuneful overture. In 1899, Mahler produced Haydn's *Lo Speziale* (*Der Apotheker*), Lortzing's *Die Opernprobe*, Siegfried Wagner's *Der Bärenhäuter* and Rubinstein's *Der Dämon*, one of the many operas which follows the *Faust* legend. The Haydn work, written in 1768, is an elegantly hilarious comic opera, and Lortzing, whose operas remain very popular in Germany was, to Mahler, next in rank after Wagner and Mozart.

Throughout his decade in Vienna, Mahler never ceased to search for new works, though the majority of those he performed did not win a permanent place in the repertoire simply because they were of limited, ephemeral appeal. He was liberal-minded enough to look for the merits of works which made no special appeal to his own taste, determined to bring to production any new worth-while work which could be adequately cast and rehearsed in the theatre he controlled; he never allowed the Opera to stagnate.

1900 brought *Iolanthe*, Tchaikovsky's last opera, a Russian fairy-tale work written in the lyrical style of his *Eugene Onegin*. In 1901 came Mahler's legendary production of *The Tales of Hoffman*, and 1902 brought *Feuersnot*, Richard Strauss's second opera and his first to make any impact on the theatre despite its being thought scandalously immoral. With it went Tchaikovsky's *Pique Dame* and Mozart's unfinished *Zaide*, a treatment of the same idea as *Die Entführung aus dem Serail*, which is its superior in emotional range and dramatic tension. Puccini's *La Bohème*, new to the Opera though not to Vienna, was given its first performance at the Opera in 1903, together with Charpentier's *Louise*. This work was popular throughout Europe and, although it was ultra-French in style and atmosphere and entirely remote from Mahler's usual preoccupations, he fell in love with it.

The only novelty of 1904 was Hugo Wolf's *Der Corregidor*. Shortly before his final mental collapse, the composer had offered it to his one-time friend and Mahler, noticing its lack of dramatic effect, had tactfully refused it on the grounds of a crowded schedule and the unavailability of suitable singers. Its belated performance was, perhaps, an act of homage after Wolf's death, in 1903. In 1905 Mahler introduced Hans Pfitzner's *Die Rose vom Liebesgarten*, which had won no great success when it had been produced at Elberfeld in 1901. Mahler's production established Pfitzner as a composer to be reckoned with in Germany, where his operas have since won devoted audiences. Mahler, at first doubtful, grew very fond of *Die Rose vom Liebesgarten* though originally he had rejected it. He reversed his decision only because his wife pleaded for its production. 'Of all the important works he was responsible for staging,' writes Marcel Prawy, 'only *Tosca*, *Tiefland* and *Pelléas* really eluded him.

'The new works he put on, were, on the whole, really less epoch-making than his revivals', Prawy notes while reckoning up Mahler's few failures. The list, however, shows two things: that Mahler did not regard himself as curator of a museum for the music of the past, and that his tastes were anything but precious or conventionally intellectual. The *Tales of Hoffman* is a work which 'serious' music-lovers tend to dismiss as too light-weight for the dignity of a great theatre. In Mahler's hands it became a masterpiece in which lightness was combined with passion and intensity and in which disturbing insights were clothed in a romantic fantasy. The search for new works, his openness to music from his Italian contemporaries and his enthusiasm for the operas of Tchaikovsky did not, of course, silence the critics who complained that he offered too many foreign novelties and did too little to encourage new German composers. Yet only *Feuersnot*, among all the new German operas which Mahler produced, has sufficient vitality to engage the minds of a modern audience, and even so its promise is more exciting than its achievement. Great operas are, after all, rare events, and Strauss's *Salome*, the greatest German opera of the Mahler decade, was banned in Vienna.

Perhaps Mahler's greatest work at the Vienna Opera was his establishment of Mozart as a great musical dramatist and not simply as a purveyor of charm and elegance. It is not, perhaps, exaggerating Mahler's influence to see his productions of the Mozart operas as the beginning of the revaluation of the composer which has led to Mozart's dominating position in twentieth-century music. The nineteenth century loved Mozartian grace, charm and melodic fertility but Mahler, who had won the support of Brahms through the strength and intensity of his Budapest *Don Giovanni*, rediscovered the passionate, 'demonic', dramatic Mozart. His contemporaries noted this quality to a lesser extent in Mahler's conducting of the symphonies, but it was with his performance of the operas he truly revealed the overwhelming stature of Mozart. In 1897 Mahler achieved a *Marriage of Figaro* shorn of the irrelevant embellishments and cadenzas that it had acquired during the nineteenth century. He

produced it not as a charming fairy tale but as social comedy, with real dramatic conflict and a strong sense of social reality. Mahler's passion for clarity led him to return to Beaumarchais's play, the source of the libretto, and add the scene in which Figaro is brought to trial for breach of promise to marry Marcellina so that the audience should clearly understand what was going on at the beginning of Act Three. The new scene was set by Mahler in *secco* recitative, with themes from the opera woven like Wagnerian *Leitmotife* into the keyboard accompaniment, and it led up to the marvellous ensemble in which Figaro discovers that Marcellina is his long-lost mother.

At first, Mahler accompanied Mozartian recitative at the piano, but after a few years in Vienna he replaced the piano with a harpsichord for the sake of authenticity—a notable innovation at that time. Typically, he forbade the addition of any notes to those which Mozart had written, so that the stylistically justifiable decoration of repeats was banned and the use of appoggiatura, which Mozart took for granted, was not allowed. Yet in his search for clarity, he was quite prepared to add and subtract. Mahler's revival of *Così fan Tutte* is a case in point. Mozart's last Italian comedy was neglected and misunderstood in the nineteenth century, which failed to see the point of its combination of a far from innocent irony with the utmost sensuous beauty, but *Così fan Tutte*, with its amused but compassionate view of sexual love, appealed deeply to the ironist in Mahler.

Though it is a long opera, Mahler omitted only two arias while suggesting possible cuts elsewhere in the score; other conductors and producers do the same sort of thing far more ruthlessly. At the same time, however, he brought in the finale of one of Mozart's Divertimenti (K.287) to give an instrumental introduction to act two and, just as he had done when he added a scene from Beaumarchais's play to *The Marriage of Figaro*, he took care that ironies should not be overlooked, heavily underlining the subtleties of the work.

To modern ears, Mozart's orchestration is faultless in balance, clarity and beauty, so that it is difficult to appreciate Mahler's 'retouchings' of the orchestration of *Così fan Tutte*. Sometimes this was done for dynamic effect; as he used the full weight of the orchestral strings in the performance, the reduction of the number

Above: A contemporary cartoon of the composer Previous page: Watching late-comers take their places. Mahler's scowl and stare were designed to induce a feeling of shame in the unpunctual. Below: A cartoon showing Mahler conducting

Below: The concert hall of the Gesellschaft der Musikfreunde *(Philharmonic Society), Vienna, in which Mahler conducted the concertos of the Vienna Philharmonic Orchestra*

of players involved during a Mozart *pianissimo* would obviously be effective. Some changes, it seems, were made from his dislike of what he considered unnecessary doublings, as when a high soprano melody is doubled with a bassoon an octave below. In the dense scoring of late nineteenth-century music, doublings of this nature tended to break Mahler's golden rule of clarity, but in Mozart's lighter, transparent orchestration, such a use of the bassoon in its high tenor register makes a colourful, typically Mozartian effect.

Though Mahler 'retouched' Mozart's orchestration and took a movement from an early Divertimento to make an introduction to the second movement, his devotion to Mozart's music cannot be questioned. As he felt he could not trust conductors to sense for themselves anything that was not set down in black and white upon the scores they used, dynamic shadings between main and subsidiary voices in the orchestra and the most minute variations of dynamic level were noted with absolute precision. Just as he was determined to create a true tradition of performance for his own works, and to lay the foundations of a new Wagnerian tradition, so he was determined to do the same for Mozart's operas. Behind everything lay his belief in the greatness of Mozart's music. His edition of *The Marriage of Figaro* was published in 1906.

Nothing for which Mahler was responsible was left to chance. He even supervised the new translations of libretti into German, insisting that all works at the Opera should be in that language unless Italian stars had been engaged for special productions. He himself actually rewrote the libretti of Weber's operas *Euryanthe*, which he regarded as magnificent music chained to Romantic absurdities, and *Oberon*, the fairy opera written for Covent Garden. He was particularly concerned about the accuracy of manner and style of libretti used for Tchaikovsky's *Pique Dame* and Verdi's *Otello* and *Tosca* which, like the new translations of Mozart's Italian operas, had been made by the Viennese critic and poet Max Kalbeck. It is interesting to note, however, that even the arch purist Mahler recognized that some arias were so firmly associated with a traditional German text that they should be left undisturbed.

Interference with the work of Mozart caused no great stir; for one thing, it was not publicized. Mahler's admission that he had 'retouched'

even the orchestration of Beethoven, however, caused a great scandal. In fact Wagner initiated this particular line in 'improving' the masterpieces of the past. He suggested that Beethoven's orchestration had been robbed of its full expressive power by the acoustic limitations of the natural, valveless horns and trumpets of his day. In its lower register their range lacked several notes so that they were unable to follow all the movements of the harmony. Many conductors had followed Wagner's lead in adding the voices of trumpets and horns where Beethoven had been compelled, apparently through the deficiency of the instruments, to use them inconsistently; and this is precisely what Mahler did. But he unwisely made a public explanation of his procedures in a programme note. The average concert-goer, who had never realized that conductors took liberties with the great Beethoven, was shocked; Mahler's opponents wantonly misrepresented the case and dubbed him a dangerous modernist.

The programme note, for a concert in February 1900, stated what were considered by many the problems of presenting Beethoven's symphonies. Because his deafness had robbed him of 'the very necessary intimate contact with physical sound' at the time when his creative development demanded new ways of expression he had evolved a more 'drastic' (a favourite Mahlerian adjective) style of orchestration. The insight of the interpretative musician was far more important for a truthful performance than simply rethinking details of orchestration. The problem was exacerbated, he continued, 'by the nature of the brass instruments, which excluded the proper formation of successive chords. This very reason had led to their improvement, and it would be a crime not to use them in order to give more perfect renderings of Beethoven's works'. He had not, he declared, re-orchestrated Beethoven's music. Mahler claimed only to have followed Wagner's teaching by filling arbitrary gaps in Beethoven's brass parts and by building up the wind sections in order to put them in proper proportion to the strings. 'In the days of Beethoven' Mahler had said in 1899, 'the entire orchestra was smaller than a modern string section. If we do not bring the other instruments into a proper numerical relationship with the strings, we cannot possibly expect to get the right effect'.

Mahler claimed that anyone who studied the scores would see that he was concerned only to carry out Beethoven's wishes and that he had allowed neither tradition nor his own intentions to come between his performance and the music itself. It rather looks as though his unhappy relationship with the orchestra had sparked off rumours that he intended sacrilege to Beethoven and this programme note was to justify himself by showing that he intended no more than was already common practice. However his performance of the String Quartet (opus 94) as a work for string orchestra on the quite subjective grounds that Beethoven's score was by its nature orchestral rather than quartet music was far more questionable. In this instance the outraged response of the orchestra and critics was justified.

Mahler's rescorings of Schumann's symphonies were more generally accepted. His adjustments and modifications of these works were accepted from the start by those who heard them, as doing more justice to the music than Schumann himself was able to do. Schumann never knew the orchestra intimately, and though careful, sympathetic conducting can bring the symphonies to life, Mahler's versions lightened thickly overscored passages, with heavily doubled themes; and revealed orchestral colours in passages which were blurred by the composer's clumsiness in the handling of instruments. Mahler simply set out to realize Schumann's aims, and though he occasionally rephrased a theme for the sake of greater effectiveness, he neither added to nor subtracted from the content of the symphonies. There is no point where he forced Schumann to speak with the voice of Mahler, for his re-orchestrations, still unfortunately unpublished, are not the works of his creative genius but of his intense interpretative imagination as a conductor.

By 1902, the musical side of Mahler's revolution in his work at the Vienna Opera was complete. In place of a number of individual virtuosi singers he had trained a group of singing actors who accepted the discipline of the ensemble and whose music was completely integrated into the dramatic plan and the musical texture. His productions were still regarded as controversial, but their vitality and conviction won far more admirers than opponents. He was still high-handed and thought nothing of cancelling a first performance at a day's notice if he felt that the new production was not up to standard. Charpentier's *Louise*

was ready for its première early in 1903 when the composer himself arrived and decided that the naturalistic settings which had been prepared for the work were not what the music required. Without a qualm Mahler cancelled the productions until new designs approved by the composer should be ready.

The Mahlerian view of opera as essentially dramatic was in the air. Toscanini, for example, seems to have disliked Mahler's conducting as heartily as he disliked the conducting of all his contemporaries, but at La Scala he carried out reforms which ran on lines parallel to those of Mahler. It was, however, Mahler's work in Vienna, at the centre of the musical tradition, which permanently changed the nature of operatic production and led to the presentation of all opera as drama rather than as a concert with scenery and costumes. Wagner had seen himself as the creator of a new, essentially dramatic art form towards which his greatest predecessors had worked as well as they could. But he believed their works had been superseded by his own, and were irrelevant to whatever standards he erected for the future. By contrast Mahler, despite his worship of Wagner, saw Wagnerian music-drama as the continuation of a German dramatic tradition which included the works of Gluck, Mozart and Weber. For him, it was the tradition that was essentially dramatic rather than any one modern composer, and every opera in that tradition needed to be produced with proper care for its theatrical qualities.

His contacts with the artistic world of Vienna made it natural for Mahler to meet Alred Roller, a painter in the Viennese Secession movement (artists who, in 1897, had seceded from outmoded academic standards and principles). Roller had become interested in matters of stage design and lighting and at their meeting in 1901, he described to Mahler his ideas for a production of Wagner's *Tristan und Isolde*. The composer was so impressed that he immediately commissioned Roller to design a new production of the work.

Wagner's stage directions, giving detailed instructions in all of his scores, were based on what had been advanced stage technique in the 1850s and '60s, the years in which he had worked out his theory of opera and planned *The Ring*, *Tristan und Isolde* and *The Master-singers*. The technique was essentially naturalistic and rooted in realism. Yet it presented

Above: The composer Hugo Wolf was a close friend of Mahler in their student days.

Below: Mahler 'reviving' Mozart's operas (with the score of Don Giovanni *trampled under his feet)*

designers, producers and actors with precise and very heavy demands. Stage mountains were to be carefully organized heaps of apparent rock or exactly painted on a back cloth; buildings were to reproduce the typical features of the architecture of the opera's period, and to be furnished with whatever could be expected to be found in them; *The Mastersingers* had to belong recognizably to Nuremburg and the Chapel of the Grail in *Parsifal* was to be an idealized version of the cathedral in Siena. So long as Cosima Wagner ruled Bayreuth, her husband's word was law. But Roller had been fired by the ideas of the Swiss stage designer Adolph Appia, published in 1889 as *Die Musik und die Inszenierung (Music and Stage Design)*. Appia set out to show that Wagner's dramatic aims could be more completely realized through production methods based on imaginative suggestion and varied, non-representational lighting than through blind obedience to an old-fashioned naturalism.

The *Tristan und Isolde* designed by Roller and produced by Mahler in 1903 proved to the Director that he had found the collaborator he wanted. It set a new standard for the visual treatment of the repertoire of the Vienna Opera. Instead of the precisely reproduced deck, bridge and cabin which Wagner demanded for Act One, a suggestion of mast and rigging was enough to set the audience's imagination to work and create the ship in their minds. A wall with a door and descending steps to the level of the stage was enough for the Garden of Act Two; a wall and a suggestion of a tower evoked Tristan's castle in Act Three. Wagner's list of properties demanded everything that a ship's cabin, a royal garden or a knightly castle might be expected to contain. In stark contrast Roller allowed nothing on to the stage unless it had some direct function in the action; Wagner's drama of symbol and allegory was not to be cluttered up with sets crowded with dramatically irrelevant furnishings. The lighting too was expressive, not naturalistic—Act One was played under glaring orange-yellow lights suggesting harsh sunshine and the 'hateful day' of which the two lovers sing; Act Two the night of would-be fulfilment, was lit by deep, luxurious violet, while the third act was suffused with an unrelieved grey light. In this style such objects as did remain on the unwontedly bare stage were given colour by the lighting and thus made responsive to the mood the designer created.

In the controversy which inevitably followed the production, Roller was accused of everything from blasphemy against Wagner to plunging the stage into inexpressive darkness. But Mahler, having approved the *Tristan* settings, promptly gave Roller a contract. The outcome was a series of revolutionary, and eventually very influential, stage settings of classics in the opera repertory. Use of a varied lighting plot in the 1905 production of *Das Rheingold* made it possible to play the work as Wagner intended, without a break after the the central Nibelung scene. The Valkyrie rode across a sky of ever-changing cloud shapes, seared by dramatic flashes of lightning. In Roller's settings for Weber's *Der Freischütz* the cosy eeriness of the Wolf's Glen became no more than an interplay of clouds, lights and shadows, disappointing the old-fashioned, who had grown fond of a more traditional spookiness.

His *Fidelio* designs concentrated on the meaning of the work in a way which must have been most unsettling for the audience. The prisoners, watched by furtive guards from the shadows, crept out for their exercise period through a low, narrow doorway as if emerging from a crack in the earth. It is not surprising that, in a century overshadowed by the horrors of the concentration camp, this prophetic image is still used by some designers for Beethoven's great opera to freedom. It was Roller's designs which prompted the beginning of the Mahler tradition of playing the *Leonora* Number 3 Overture between the two scenes of Act Two. Mahler had previously used that Overture as an introduction to Act Two (a practice which displeased some London critics in 1902), but Roller's scene change in Act Two needed no curtain; it was designed as a transformation scene, and Mahler began to use the *Leonora* Number 3 as an entr'acte. Possibly he did so at first as a purely practical measure, to bridge the time taken by the scene change; however he came to defend the new practice on artistic grounds as providing a necessary musical transition from the dungeon scene to the rapturous music of liberation in the finale.

Roller's moves toward the concept of a permanent set, so common in modern stage design, proved equally disturbing. In *Don Giovanni*, the stage throughout the performance was dominated by two towers, seemingly of grey stone, which could be set in different positions on the stage. At the beginning of the opera they were the Commendatore's house, in the graveyard scene imposing monuments. At times they revealed windows which were sometimes curtained, sometimes no more than blank openings in high walls; sometimes, with brilliant lighting, they showed luxuriously furnished rooms. Like the revolving stage, which Mahler first used in *Così fan Tutte*, they speeded up the action and helped to preserve a sense of unity in the action. Mahler demanded their use again in a new production of *Die Entführung aus dem Serail*; quite apart from giving unity of atmosphere to the work, they had the merit of cutting the cost of the production. Though 1904 was a financial high-water mark in the history of the Imperial Opera, with a profit of 48,900 kroner for the season of 1903–4, Mahler remained as cautious as ever in his supervision of finance.

The years in Vienna were fantastically active. Mahler was responsible for an annual repertory of some fifty-four operas, regularly introducing totally new productions, and had composed the Fourth, Fifth, Sixth, Seventh and Eighth Symphonies. Yet there was a persistent personal campaign against him. Any interpretative artist of great personal force and originality will inevitably infuriate some people while delighting others, but Mahler's arrogance of manner, his unbending will-power, his disregard for others and his contempt for opponents whatever their grounds of opposition inevitably made him many enemies in the musical world. Singers whose appetite for publicity was greater than their loyalty to him and to the theatre, happily retailed highly coloured accounts of rehearsal squabbles. Such tittle-tattle made welcome news items, and 'Another incident at the Opera' was a familiar Viennese headline during the Mahler decade. The private man, generous, affectionate and lovable, remained incredibly distant from the haughty and controversial Opera Director.

But so long as he made the opera profitable and filled the theatre with capacity audiences, Mahler's position was secure—a fact that he never realized. In 1901 when he first thought of marriage, he told Alma that his job at the opera was only 'from day to day'. After 1904, profits began to fall. To what extent his determined backing of Roller's new ideas contributed to their decline it is not possible to say, nor can we estimate the effects of the increasing number of invitations Mahler received to conduct his own

works in other cities. When, refusing to accept external authority, he had threatened resignation over the banning of Strauss's *Salome* in 1905, his resignation had been refused. Two years later, the authorities were ready to create the situation in which he could be expected to resign.

His career as a composer had again come into conflict with his official duties; his frequent absences from Vienna to conduct his own works, brief though they were when compared to the latitude modern conductors enjoy, provided the opera staff with cause for complaint. Secondly, though he had always observed rules and official courtesies punctiliously, he was led into breaches of regulation by his support of all Roller's schemes even when the designer announced his determination to produce a ballet and entered into open conflict with the ballet master. It became impossible for Prince Montenuovo, despite his respect for Mahler and as near an approach to friendliness as a rigidly chilly aristocrat could feel for a mere musician, to disregard formal complaints against Mahler by members of the company.

Mahler's opponents knew him well enough to realize that his response to reprimand and formal complaint would be resignation, as it had been under similar circumstances in Leipzig. Mahler was convinced that everything he had done in Vienna had been motivated by the highest musical principles and that he had done nothing blameworthy. Montenuovo pointed out that his absences from Vienna were harming the Opera because takings always fell when he was absent; Mahler refused to accept this and declared that, on the contrary, the prestige of the Opera rose if its Director had a reputation for original work. His enemies knew him well enough to feel sure that if he were faced with the choice between his position in Vienna and his task of introducing his music to the world, it was Vienna that would suffer. No one but he could conduct his music as it should be conducted, and he had a duty to his destiny to see that his works were properly presented to the public. His enemies knew that any compromise would be unacceptable to him.

Furthermore, he had come to believe that he had done all that could be done in Vienna, but that his efforts had been a failure. True he had set a new, exalted standard of performance both for the music and for all the visual elements of opera. But, in the detested framework of the

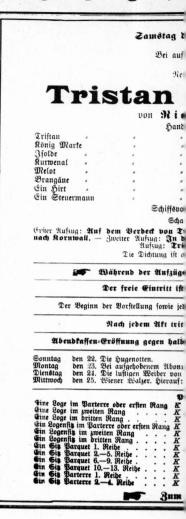

The announcement of the production of Wagner's Tristan und Isolde *first seen on 21st February 1903. This was the beginning of the collaboration between Mahler and Alfred Roller which revolutionized the staging of opera*

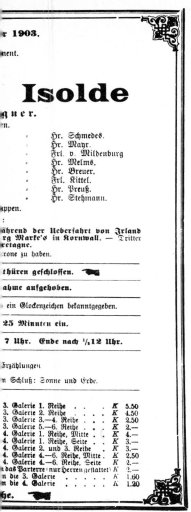

repertory system, though his work was done, the system had triumphed; while nobody could raise the Opera to greater heights, it was still enslaved by routine. The only hope for Opera was that it should be saved for festival performances to which artists and audiences, unstaled by routine, would carry their enthusiasm and love of each work to the service of music and not merely to the pleasure of an audience.

Reprimanded and criticized, personally though unreasonably disillusioned with the results of ten years of historic achievement, Mahler resigned his post. There was no negotiation, no effort to accommodate his need for greater freedom to the demands of the theatre. Negotiation would have meant compromise and was not therefore considered because it implied the possibility that the principles which had motivated him had been wrong. Montenuovo's difficulty was to find a successor capable of measuring up to Mahler's powerful personality, his fanatical appetite for work and his sacrificial, dedicated musicianship. When he had failed to find another Mahler, he asked that the resignation be withdrawn. He was willing to agree that Mahler's growing fame as a composer, although it meant occasional absence from Vienna, was beneficial to the Opera and to concede Mahler's right to accept invitations to conduct elsewhere. It might be possible to increase his opportunities for travel, but by that time the Director had already accepted an engagement to conduct the German repertory at the Metropolitan Opera House, New York, and told Montenuovo that he had come to accept the Court Chamberlain's point of view: the Director of the Opera should be a man free to devote his time exclusively to it. Montenuovo had been compelled by Mahler's opponents to engage in a trial of strength with the conductor, and Mahler had won it, but at what he came to realize as a heavy loss to himself.

Though he put all his Austrian decorations into a draw of the Director's desk, 'for the use of my successor', and described himself as 'the man who had been sacked,' his departure was his own doing. He had followed the principle that his carefully worked out, devotedly held principles were right, to its logical conclusion where criticism was entirely unacceptable.

His last performance at the Vienna Opera House was on 15 October 1907. It was as though the spell had been broken, for the campaign of hostility had intensified once the news of Mahler's departure became public. For the only time during his years at Vienna, he conducted to a poor audience. A group of eminent writers, painters, artists and musicians petitioned the Court Intendent to retain him, but the resignation took effect on 1 December 1907. Nevertheless, Mahler was awarded a higher annual pension than went with his post, a grant of 20,000 kroner in compensation for his loss of office, and for Alma after his death a pension equal to that of a Privy Councillor.

Mahler's letter of farewell to the company was particularly naïve. He seems to have been sublimely unaware that he had made lasting enemies or that he had unforgivably hurt and humiliated many of his subordinates. He wrote:

The time has come to end our collaboration. I have to leave the workshop I have come to love, and to say farewell to you. Instead of achieving something whole and perfect, as I had dreamed of doing, everything I leave behind is incomplete, imperfect; such is the fate of humanity. It is not up to me to judge those people who have come to appreciate my work and to whom it was dedicated.

His original German is as obscure as any translation; he was, perhaps, eager to show that he left Vienna with no personal resentments, forgiving his opponents and softening their bitter criticism into the word 'appreciate'.

Nevertheless, I may assure them at this moment that I always meant well and aimed high. I did not always succeed. Any practising artist is in more danger than anyone else of falling victim to the 'intractability of the material'. But I always dedicated all my strength to subordinating myself to the subject and my inclinations to my duty. I never spared myself and therefore I felt justified in asking the utmost from others. In the heat of the conflict I could not avoid mistakes and injuries. But when we reached our goal and solved our problems, we forgot our differences and unhappiness; we felt richly rewarded even when we saw no outward sign of success. We all advanced, and this institution, to which we dedicated all our efforts, advanced with us. I give my heartfelt thanks to everyone who aided me in this difficult, often thankless task, who assisted me and struggled beside me. Please accept my good wishes for your future and the prosperity of the Imperial Opera . . .

Mahler's farewell was pinned to the notice board on the day of his departure for all to read. By the following day, it had been torn into small pieces and the fragments, in a gesture of contempt, reaffixed to the board.

Chapter 6

American Postscript

In New York, Mahler's job was to conduct only the German repertoire of the Metropolitan Opera. A few years drudgery there, he believed, would enable him to retire and devote his time entirely to composition; there would be no struggles except those inevitable in the attempt to secure satisfactory performances. He acquiesced in practices which he had formerly found unbearable; even making no protest against the then conventional cuts in the operas of Wagner. It was not that he had mellowed, but simply that he had come to the conclusion that repertory opera was incurably faulty and not worth fighting over. In New York, he would at any rate be spared anti-semitic lunacies: 'I'm going to America because I can't stand the mob any longer,' he said in June 1907, when his negotiations with Conreid, the Director of the New York Metropolitan, settled his immediate future. But he soon found that work in an Opera House that depended on the goodwill of wealthy subscribers was difficult; he was not good at wooing rather than ruling an audience, while his constitutional inability to accept any situation as he found it led him to try to win Roller from Vienna to work beside him in New York. He was not designed by nature to be a subordinate and looked for a colleague to help him to make changes.

His first Metropolitan season occupied the first four months of 1908, and he opened it with a performance of *Tristan und Isolde* on 2 January; the critic of *The New York Times*, Richard Aldrich, wrote:

The influence of the new conductor was felt and heard in the whole spirit of the performance. . . . His tempi were frequently somewhat quicker than we have been accustomed to; and they were always such as to fill the music with dramatic life. They were elastic and full of subtle variations. Most striking was the firm hand with which he kept the volume of orchestral sound controlled and subordinated to the voices. They were never overwhelmed; the balance was never lost and they were

allowed to keep their place above the orchestra and blend with it always in their rightful place. And yet the score was revealed in all its complex beauty. . . .

A month later, heralding his visit to Boston with the Metropolitan Company, an article signed 'H.J.P.' in *The Boston Evening Transcript* offered a glowing character sketch based on an account of his work in Vienna; it described his appearance and manner, noting the absolute control he exercised over the orchestra with the minimum of gesture:

With one hand he gently but explicitly plies his stick; the other lies loosely in his lap. With that stick he indicates pace, rhythm and accent, while with his left hand he heightens or lessens the volume of sound. It is with his eyes, seemingly, that he conducts.

The power and dramatic passion which he released with such slight physical effort had a profound effect upon Aldrich, whose writings suggest that in America Mahler was still at his high point of insight and authority. His two Metropolitan seasons in 1908 and 1909 were a popular and a critical success, but Conreid's determination to bring another star conductor to the Metropolitan, Toscanini, could only be achieved if Toscanini were allowed to conduct *Tristan*. So Mahler, without any strong ties to the Opera House, resigned after two seasons and Toscanini began his reign in New York by pouring scorn over Mahler's interpretation of *Tristan und Isolde*.

But Mahler was offered a new engagement which he found more attractive than his limited authority at the Metropolitan; it would subject him to no control, he believed, so that he would not be forced into artistic compromises. The New York Philharmonic Orchestra, founded in 1842 as a self-governing body, had suffered from the competition of the New York Symphony Orchestra, which Walter Damrosch had founded in 1878. In the season of 1908-9, it was faced with extinction unless its members

Above: Mahler, a cartoon by the famous tenor Enrico Caruso
Right: The stage set of Act One of Tristan und Isolde *as Mahler conducted the work at the Metropolitan Opera House, New York in 1908*

shared control with an outside body. With a guarantee of 90,000 dollars for three years and a committee of management composed of wealthy business men and representatives of the orchestra, it offered Mahler the post of conductor and artistic director.

Typically, he accepted with optimistic enthusiasm; for the first time in his career he was to have his own concert orchestra and the dictatorial powers without which he believed effective work to be impossible. He took the orchestra through a Beethoven cycle and a series of 'Historical Concerts', and made its general programmes more adventurous, compensating for any strain on the audience's patience by inaugurating the more popular Sunday afternoon concerts which, twenty years later, were to become enormously important to a wider audience through their regular radio transmission. He toured extensively, at incalculable risk to his health, accepting a missionary role by taking music where an orchestra had rarely been heard before. Among the works unfamiliar to American audiences which he made it his business to perform were Elgar's *Enigma Variations* and *Sea Pictures*, and Debussy's *Rondes de Printemps* and *Iberia*. He was, he knew, a man under sentence of death, but his interest in the new and the exploratory had not diminished.

Richard Aldrich studied Mahler's conducting style at length in a notice of his first New York concert on 30 November 1908:

No conductor is less concerned with the pictorial impression he makes upon the listeners, or is more concentrated upon the business of the orchestra than Mr Mahler. He has absolutely none of the graces, none of the poses or ornate, unnecessary gestures of the '*prima donna*' conductor as he stands upon the platform, short in stature, without distinction of figure or manner, with left hand occasionally thrust into his pocket. His beat is usually short, decisive and very clear; his motions are all for the orchestra, without graphic or picturesque significance for the eye of the listener. But the intense energy, the keenness and penetration, the force and authority of the man were an electric stimulus to the players.

Mahler made no effort, Aldrich wrote, to impose his personality on the music or exploit it for his personal glory; naturally the performance was 'conditioned by the personality of the conductor', but Mahler was 'one who seeks always sincerely for the spirit of the composer through a natural and elegant utterance.' The performances were balanced, mature, uneccentric, without 'anxious searching for "expression".' It was to the warmth, sincerity, vitality and rhythmic life of the music that Mahler drew attention.

But there were the inevitable Mahlerian storms. The New York Philharmonic became another hostile force to be broken to his will. One of its members (according to Alma

Mahler) became his friend by describing his sufferings from consumption, and once in Mahler's confidence he enhanced his importance to the conductor by discussing the failings and disloyalties of his colleagues. At the same time, in place of a Director he had a Ladies' Committee which, through its members' lavish support of the orchestra, acted as though each of its members was his employer. The Committee wished to draw up the programmes he should play, and Mahler at first indulged them, only to find himself faced with demands for music in which he had lost interest, and then with a bitter struggle to extricate himself. He never learnt the art, quickly acquired by Stokowski a few years later, of mastering a Ladies Committee through a devastating combination of bullying, charm and cajolery.

Summers, and what seemed like his real life, were spent in Europe, where, in 1910, came the greatest triumph of his career. The Eighth Symphony, completed three years before, was given its first performance in the Musikfesthalle, a new building in Munich. The vast forces necessary were assembled and the hall booked to capacity when Mahler arrived and, by a typical piece of tactlessness, imperilled the entire operation. Unsure of the quality of the leader of the Munich Orchestra, he sent for his

brother-in-law, Alfred Rosé, from Vienna, to lead, and only Rosé's tactful, dignified withdrawal from an untenable position prevented Mahler from fatally antagonizing the orchestra. The huge work came to life on 12 September 1910, with Mahler conducting—tiny, restrained in gesture, controlling his armies with hardly a movement of his left hand. For the only time in his life, he heard one of his works accepted with unanimous acclamation.

Six months later, on 21 February, he conducted his last concert in New York, collapsed and was brought back to Vienna, where he died on 18 May 1911. Hearing the news, Richard Strauss interrupted one of his business-like, common-sense letters to his librettist, Hugo von Hofmannsthal (they were busy with *Ariadne auf Naxos*) with a few words about Mahler.

Mahler's death was a great blow to me. Now you'll find that even the Viennese will realise that Mahler was a great man.

Vienna did so; his funeral cortege passed, like the funeral processions of Haydn and Beethoven, through streets lined with mourners. Mahler, it seems, had to die to be loved by his public.

Above: An announcement, listing soloists, combined choirs of 850 voices and orchestra of 150

Left: The Music Festival Hall of the Exhibition Buildings, Munich, where the Eighth Symphony was performed to inaugurate the hall

Chapter 7

The Composer at Work

Mahler's professional commitments as a conductor were so demanding that it is something of a marvel that he found time for composing at all. His working day during the operatic seasons at Hamburg and Vienna have been described for us by Natalie Bauer-Lechner and the composer's wife. He began the day early reading a book over breakfast; then came administrative work followed by a rehearsal. After lunch he took the orchestra in the afternoon rehearsal and perhaps had another session in the office before preparing for the evening performance. Each production was meticulously prepared, whether it was a regular feature of the repertory or an entirely new work; in the first case Mahler thoroughly revised the work and in the second case he went to endless pains to make sure that he had an intimate understanding of the new opera before putting it into rehearsal. He worked to a taxing schedule in the theatre and yet, between his arrival at Hamburg in 1891 and his death twenty years later, he completed the Second Symphony, wrote most of the songs in the *Knaben Wunderhorn Cycle*, the Rückert Songs the *Kindertotenlieder*, *The Song of the Earth* and all the other symphonies.

After his appointment to Hamburg, Mahler described himself almost contemptuously as a 'Summer holiday composer', which means that he must have worked with enormous speed and assurance during those holidays. The only work he composed in relative freedom from pressure was the early *Das klagende Lied*. The four *Lieder eines fahrenden Gesellen* (*Songs of a Wayfarer*) occupied him from 1883 to the beginning of 1885, the First Symphony from 1884 to 1888. The Second was probably begun in 1887 and was not completed until 1894, not because he worked at it slowly but because for long he could not find the right text for the words of affirmation which he wanted in the finale.

As a young assistant conductor, Mahler's composition was slow because he had not discovered the way in which to organize his life. The First Symphony was finished only because he allowed it to distract him from his official duties in Leipzig; like the *Lieder eines fahrenden Gesellen*, it was written whenever he could find the time.

Vienna and a more carefully organized life with few administrative duties, both forced him to divide his time between conducting and composition. He left town when the opera season ended, moved to his holiday home and devoted himself to composition. Each of his summer homes—Steinbach am Attersee until 1901, then Maiernigg in Carinthia and then, after the death of his daughter, Toblach—provided him with a small detached summer house some distance from his companions. There, with a piano, Bach's *Well-Tempered Clavier* as the only essential music and with a few equally essential books, he shut himself away from the world and worked. Any interruption was forbidden on 'pain of death'. While he was working, dogs, cats and even farmyard birds in his neighbourhood were expected to keep silent and he fought a real war with the crows. On one of her visits Natalie Bauer-Lechner noted that Mahler spent most of his time in what he called his *Schnützelputz-Häusel*, his 'little gingerbread house'. One day at Maiernigg, a piano salesman called at the house during his working hours and a cook, too new to be used to Mahler's habits, showed the salesman where he was. The salesman attempted to attract his attention with a stentorian bellow, ruining Mahler's temper and the rest of his working day.

From eight till twelve, during Natalie Bauer-Lechner's visits, he worked with such intensity that his nervous irritability when he emerged seemed quite natural. For an hour, before lunch at one, he went for a solitary walk to bring his mind down to earth. Later he would walk or cycle, but his mind was rarely far from composition. He would drop behind, take out a notebook and begin to write, but his companions were not allowed to notice what he was doing. Even when he was a married man, the appearance of the notebook and pencil during a walk was something Alma was supposed not to notice.

The piano in his workshop was not to aid composition. The music was already in his head and his hours there were spent getting it accurately on to paper in short score, that is to say on two staves as though it were piano music. Only when the sketch of a movement was complete did he stop to play it on the piano and correct anything that he found unsatisfactory. After a movement had been completed in rough it was worked up into a more elaborate orchestral sketch. At the end of the summer, whatever he had written went back with him to town to be turned into an orchestral score during the uncreative winter.

Working up the orchestral sketch and full score was not a process involving creative decisions as to the appropriate instruments for the music noted during the creative summer sessions. Mahler did not conceive music in the abstract and then consider which instruments would express it most effectively. On the contrary, he composed for the orchestra from the first moment, mentally hearing the instruments he needed. While his original sketch did not set out to be complete, it contained the whole substance and structure of a movement. In some places the sketch might run on for a number of bars simply as a single melodic thread; at others it might convey the whole of a complex passage. The second orchestral sketch noted the entire harmony and texture so that the writing of the orchestral score became only a necessary, rather mechanical chore; though it also provided an opportunity for revision.

In the full score he took the greatest care to ensure that his intentions were exactly carried out in performance. 'If, for instance, two consecutive notes have to be played separately to sound meaningful,' he noted in 1895, 'I don't rely on the understanding of the conductor. I give one note to the first violins and one to the seconds rather than ask either first or seconds play both. If I want one voice subdued, I allow only one, two or three desks to sound, according to my requirements. I only use all desks when their full strength is required.' The musical architect-poet presided over the creation of the sketch-score; the full score was in the hands of his *alter ego*, a consummate craftsman.

'To make any alteration of the rhythm impossible,' he continued, 'I do my utmost to make everything as detailed as may be. For instance, I avoid using *staccato* signs to make the shortness of a note clear or mark the entry of a new instrument!' Rather than depend on a *staccato* sign to indicate mere brevity, he would break the melodic line with a minute rest. The absence of a *staccato* mark over the opening of a new entry avoided emphatic accentuation where it was not wanted.

The spells of intense creative work which his double career made necessary could not be carried on uninterruptedly for too long. At times he found it necessary to stop for a day or a few days so that he could stand back like a painter and see his work in perspective (the simile was his own). A break of that kind left him able to return fresh to his work and its problems. Though he did not sit down to work at a sketch during these breaks, his creative mind remained active just below the level of consciousness. His notebook went with him everywhere and it seems that almost anything— scenery, exercise itself, sometimes, perhaps, conversation—provided a necessary stimulus. The book would come from his pocket and some decisive theme, contrapuntal passage or harmony would be jotted down. On one occasion, an unusually lengthy hold-up in which work seemed impossible was ended by the rhythm of a lake steamer's engine.

Revision was an almost continuous process. Because he was evolving a new orchestral style, he would arrange a trial rehearsal of a new work as soon as he could after it was finished and adjustments, corrections and alterations were made as a result. The music had been in his mind when he wrote it down; the purpose of the trial-rehearsal was to be sure that he had set it down correctly.

Before its first performance in 1901, *Das klagende Lied* had been through four revisions. In 1888, it was 'retouched' and its first part removed; a further process of 'retouching' was carried out in 1896. In 1898, a further close scrutiny led to more modifications and adjustments of its orchestration. Mahler regarded the work as the beginning of his true career as a composer and he destroyed all that he could find of his earlier music. *Das klagende Lied* was

Above right: La Scala, Milan Right: Interior of the auditorium, State Opera House, Vienna

RODIN (Auguste)
Silon Mathor

completed when he was twenty years old, and is a work of remarkable assurance and panache, using a semi-symphonic style to convey a narrative and developing characteristic themes effectively. It was easy at one time to believe that so picturesque and colourful a score was a boy's inspiration revised into mastery by a very experienced composer-conductor.

However the manuscript of the suppressed Part One, untouched since 1888 and of the first revision, was preserved in the family of Mahler's sister, Justine, and has been recorded in recent years as well as heard in concert performances. Fundamentally, it differs hardly at all in style from the final version of Parts Two and Three. Donald Mitchell and Hans Redlich have noted that the revisions brought many minor but telling adjustments of the orchestration to increase the work's clarity. Over and above this, they note the addition of a multitude of expression marks and directions to ensure that, as far as humanly possible, conductors would understand every nuance, variation of dynamic level and fluctuation of tempo that Mahler wished to convey. To a large extent these, and the almost too explicit directions he loaded on to his later scores, were indications of his distrust of the average conductor. Some instructions dealing with, for example, the relationship

of the various *tempi* of a movement to its basic speed affected nobody but the conductor, and appear as footnotes.

Everything he wrote was subject to similar painstaking revision. Preparing one of his scores for performance, even though he had often conducted it before, led him to study it with most intense critical care and retouch anything which, he felt, could be simplified in the interests of clarity or marked on the score to give players and conductors a clearer idea of what was expected from them. Almost invariably his revisions were simplifications, many of them so minute that only ears as fastidiously acute as his own would notice their effect. Even after such thorough preparation as this, his critical vigour was still in force when he conducted the work and he might make still further corrections after the performance.

It was not the substance of his music which dissatisfied Mahler; only rarely did he find it necessary to alter the notes of a theme, modify its phrasing or make changes in harmony or the layout of his counterpoint. His revisions were almost invariably aimed at ensuring the correct presentation of the work by the orchestra. The Fifth Symphony, for example, seemed never to satisfy him. It was completed in 1902 and marked a radical development of his style. All his earlier symphonies except the First had called for voices; the Fifth is entirely orchestral and almost entirely built from the interplay of themes and motives in counterpoint. It was the first symphony written after his marriage and, perhaps because she knew it so intimately, the first which Alma Mahler came to love. After its first performance, she burst into tears and accused him of drowning the music under the noise of a battery of percussion. Mahler recognized the justice of her accusation and made three published revisions of the already revised score published in 1904. He continued to retouch and adapt its orchestration in almost every performance he conducted.

The Fifth was the most frequently and painstakingly revised of all his works, but even the sunny Fourth was revised from time to time. Mahler's last, still unpublished, revision of the work dates from 1910. The Sixth, the only one of his works which ends in utter despair, provided a different problem; he could not decide whether its bitter, sarcastic Scherzo came before or after its beautiful, lyrical Andante. He saw the Andante, first, as its second movement and then changed its place with that of the Scherzo. Two versions were published almost simultaneously, a sign of uncertainty rather than a change of mind; then, after the publication, he seems to have leaned towards the idea— 'decided' would be too strong a word—that the Scherzo should follow the Andante.

Only *Das Lied von der Erde* and the Ninth Symphony, neither performed during his lifetime, remained unrevised. One wonders whether the works in performance would have seemed so precisely and finely achieved to him as they do to us. For example, the climax of the first movement of *Das Lied*—the tenor's *Trinklied vom Jammer der Erde* (The drinking song of Earth's sorrow) forces the singer, if he is to be audible, to yell into a raging orchestral *fortissimo*. One can speculate whether, having heard the effect, Mahler would have lightened the orchestration or whether the desperate mood of the work would have convinced him, as it convinces us, that this hectic passage is the perfect expression of his meaning.

The extent of Mahler's revisions and the way in which he returned to a work time and again, are the more impressive when we consider how little time his professional schedule left him for creative composition. As a conductor he knew how much scope the scores of the past left to their interpreters and he was determined that his own should be performed as he intended.

A symphonic composer whose major works include a number of songs and song cycles is likely to provide us with more clues to the understanding of his musical language than one whose music is exclusively instrumental. From the way in which he associates words and music in his settings of other men's poems we can discover something of the way in which particular emotions or concepts present themselves to him in musical terms. If we find similar idioms in his symphonic music, we can be reasonably sure that they are intended to express similar trains of thought. Thus, from the trains of thought displayed in Mahler's songs, we can begin to attach to his symphonies the precise meanings that he set out to express.

Mahler's early songs—written before 1883 though published in 1885 and 1892—contain pleasant, conventional settings of minor romantic poems by Leander in the first book; only a setting of words by Mahler himself, a folkish *Hans und Grete*, is in any way unexpected. The songs of Books Two and Three take their texts from *Des Knaben Wunderhorn*, an anthology of German folk poetry collected by Ludwig von Arnim and Clemens Brentano and published in 1808. These are entirely prophetic of the mature Mahler. They speak a musical idiom close to folk song and demonstrate the range of his interests beyond the conventional material of the Romantic composer.

The poems in the *Knaben Wunderhorn* anthology liberated Mahler's imagination; they provided him with texts which seemed to symbolize and reflect in simple, concrete, immediately comprehensible ways large areas of the life he knew. Between 1888 and 1896 he set another ten of the poems as independent songs for voice and orchestra, and he returned to the anthology for the words set in movements of the Second, Third and Fourth Symphonies. Some of the musical ideas he found for these poems echo through his later music. *Das irdische Leben* (Earthly Life) for example—the story of a child pleading for food, fed on promises, and dying before the promises can be kept—has a restless, *moto perpetuo* style accompaniment. It suggests similar music in the scherzo of the Fourth Symphony, while it recurs in the *Purgatorio* movement of his unfinished Tenth, as though it were the type of musical figuration which came spontaneously

to his mind to portray the humdrum affairs of everyday life.

When Mahler showed the *Wunderhorn* songs to von Bülow, hoping for a performance in Hamburg, Bülow told him that they were too eccentric to be comprehensible. Their use of popular idioms, the composer's essentially symphonic development of the song melodies and the highly original quality of the orchestration, all contributed to produce an orchestral style that von Bülow, then in his sixties, found as incomprehensible as it was new. In one song, where the poet speaks of 'shining trumpets' which bring a dead soldier back to his girl friend, Mahler uses oboes instead of trumpets; when he does use trumpets they appear as often in lyrical passages as in military calls to arms. Unconventional touches such as these were to be a characteristic of Mahler's music which was eventually accepted; in the early 1890s they seemed unnecessarily perverse to at least one aging conductor.

Probably the most popular of all Mahler's songs are to be found in the cycle *Lieder eines Fahrenden Gesellen* (*Songs of a Wayfarer*) though this may only be because a cycle makes a convenient item in a concert programme. Composed between 1883 and 1885, the songs grew out of his unsuccessful love affair with Jehanne Richter.

The cycle was written for voice and orchestra though Mahler issued it first in a version for voice and piano. The orchestral version which we know, published in 1897, is apparently that of a second revision undertaken in 1896. This had been made for the concert in Berlin at which he conducted the *Lieder* as a curtain raiser to the First Symphony which uses several of its melodies. Its orchestration is economical, distinguished by clarity rather than fullness of tone; harmonically it used the technique which has come to be called 'Progressive Tonality'. In orthodox practice, a work written within the tonal system is expected to end in the key in which it began, however far it travels round the key system and whatever related keys it uses in its inner movements. *Lieder eines Fahrenden Gesellen* begins in D Minor, moves through keys not closely related to each other, three times to a key a semitone higher than the key of the last song or section (the effect is that of wrenching the music into a new area) and ends in F minor. The results of this are twofold; the complete finality we expect at the end

of any work does not arrive; we realize that the wanderer seeking happiness after an unhappy love affair will continue to wander unsatisfied. Secondly the cycle of key through which the music moves creates the effect of a progress from a state of active sorrow to a passive desire to sleep sorrow away.

The *Kindertotenlieder* (*Songs on the Death of Children*), a cycle of five songs set to poems by Friedrich Rückert in which the poet mourned the death of his children, were written between 1901 and 1904. During the same period Mahler set five other poems by Rückert but, apart from two of these that may have been inspired by his courtship of and marriage to Alma, we can trace nothing in the composer's life to account for his choice of texts. We have no clue why he should have poured so much of himself into setting music on this tragic theme that apparently had no bearing on his own situation at all. Perhaps it was a belated tribute to the long-dead but dearly loved brother Ernst.

All the songs have an orchestral accompaniment, but the orchestra is treated with the most fastidious restraint. Two of the separate songs, *Ich atmet' einen linden Duft* ('I inhaled a gentle scent') and *Ich bin der Welt abhanden gekommen* ('I am lost to the world'), seem to be written along the boundary line between sound and silence, the orchestra is used as a chamber group, two, three or four instrumental lines at a time weaving a contrapuntal pattern out of and around the voices' melody. The second song is an ecstacy of contentment: 'Lost to the world, I live alone in my heaven, my love, my song'. Its melody haunts several of Mahler's later and larger works.

The helplessly sorrowful music of *Kindertotenlieder* is equally restrained in its use of the orchestra; only the final song, in which the father blames himself for his children's death before bringing himself to accept the fact in a lullaby of heart-broken serenity, provides any sort of climax. Throughout Mahler respects the poet's stanza form, though he never allows it to dominate his conception or decide his musical style. In fact, these songs are utterly unique thanks to a number of factors; among them the most important are Mahler's characteristic use of popular music idioms and his use of orchestration. In view of the degree to which twentieth-century composers were to plunder the realms of jazz and popular music decades after Mahler, his use of this highly 'unserious' material is almost prophetic. Transformed fragments of music from the popular stage or the street ballad were to become an essential feature of the 'Mahlerian worlds' that he built up in his symphonies. His use of the technique in these songs is just one of the ways in which he married the intellectual subtleties of his symphonic developments to words, to make songs that are miniature symphonic movements.

But it is in their orchestration that Mahler's song cycles show their affinity to his symphonic music most obviously. He was a composer for whom orchestral expression seems to have been indispensable and almost unavoidable. Themes and melodies, which to other composers often appear first as abstract lines and shapes to be embellished or enriched with instrumental colour at some later date, presented themselves to Mahler from the outset in orchestral terms— as violin themes, oboe themes or perhaps trombone themes. He thought, so to speak, in colour. Like every other aspect of his work, the songs were concerned with symbolism and significance and for him instrumental colour was one of the most potent aspects of musical symbolism. Hence he employed an orchestra to accompany his songs where others were content with the piano, not because he suffered from delusions of grandeur, but because the music came to him in terms of instrumental colours which were so clear that simply to give a theme to a different instrument would have to involve some modification or development of the theme. We conclude this discussion of the symbolism of his songs with a look at his use of the orchestra, because it is also central to them as it is in the symphonies.

The originality of Mahler's orchestration is not in the range of his orchestral palette, though this is unusually wide, but in his habit of weaving a musical texture in strands of contrasted colour. Orchestration was the aspect of composition which seems to have demanded the most careful thought and working out; at any rate, it is orchestration which demanded the most subtle revision and which he was inclined to discuss in technical terms.

The cataclysmic introduction to the Second Symphony, when he described it, was not a series of contrasted themes in C minor which he intended, by the end of the movement, to show as closely related; it was, he explained, a series of agonized questions we are forced to

Previous page, above and right: Scenes from Anthony Tudor's ballet to the music of Kindertotenlieder, *danced by the Ballet Rambert, London*

ask ourselves when we consider the inevitability of death. The Third Symphony begins with a 'great laugh of the whole world' and, in its finale, 'The Ixion's wheel of outward forms is resolved into stillness. Everything becomes still.' He was surprised and delighted to find that the structure was that which he found in the symphonies of Haydn, Mozart and Beethoven. He spent a considerable time explaining to Natalie Bauer-Lechner what he 'envisioned' as he wrote the scherzo of the Fourth Symphony. When he discussed music with his wife he talked in the same way, attempting to paraphrase the 'meaning' of his works in words although he knew that the task was impossible. Originalities of style and technique were never discussed; the unprecedented audacity of such movements as the opening march of the Third Symphony seems never to have occurred to him.

The orchestral dress which belonged as if by nature to his themes often seemed to need delicate refinements and retailoring, and he talked about this earnestly and at length. Originality and beauty were forced on him by the 'meanings' he set out to express. Because the meaning grew from the relationships between the ideas and experiences which made up his symphonic worlds, his symphonies had to allow contrasting themes and motives to be heard together in counterpoint. So that they could be presented with the greatest possible clarity, he found it necessary and natural to use instruments whose voices contrasted sharply, one of the string group, for example, against one of the wood-wind and, possibly, against a horn or a trumpet. Mahler's music is full of passages in which a huge orchestra is treated like a chamber ensemble with two, or three, or even four instruments playing apparently independent lines of melody.

The 'colour' of Mahler's orchestral music is remarkable because of this. Wagner, for example, composed music in which harmony and orchestration create some passages with a sombre glow, others where the colour is brilliant or glittering, others in which it shines, fiercely or tenderly, but we feel that each mood commands a different colour and that colours do not mix. Mahler, composing often in two or more lines of counterpoint, creates the impression that each line has a colour of its own.

The essentially contrapuntal style of his music led him to use all instruments as melodic instruments. 'For me,' he said 'even the bassoon and the bass tuba, even the timpani, must sing.' Only if they did so could he find the range of instrumental colours he needed to be sure that the interplay of themes would stand out clearly enough. In a sense, too, instruments became interchangeable; one of the most beautiful of Romantic dawns breaks in the opening of the First Symphony with wood-wind playing a fanfare figure which, conventionally speaking, belongs to the trumpets; the brief cataclysmic funeral march in the first movement of the

Ninth Symphony ends with a violin fanfare. In the Second Symphony, a lyrical melody is given to the trumpets because they can penetrate the orchestral texture, and it is marked 'very, very sweetly'.

Mahler demanded huge orchestras to ensure clarity rather than to achieve power. Once the questions of balance posed by the nineteenth-century enlargement of the string section had been answered, as he had answered them in his Beethoven performances, additional instruments were added for the sake of clarity. They were often instruments conventionally excluded from the concert hall—the cowbells of the Sixth and Seventh symphonies, used as symbols of loneliness and exaltation; the celeste, harmonium, mandoline or guitar which he occasionally demanded elsewhere—but they were never called in simply to add to a climax, but only because they extended his expressive palette.

Mahler was also a master of conventional orchestration. When instruments are meant to be prominent, he writes for them in the register in which they are most effective; violins are sonorously eloquent on their lowest string, beautiful, emotional and affecting on their highest; the almost screaming tone of oboes high in their register can be heard above the stressful, strong orchestral *tutti*. Mahler's inventiveness with the orchestra is revealed by the unusual combinations of familiar instruments as well as the more rarely heard xylophone, Glockenspiel and celeste or harp. The harp is distinctive, of course, in almost any orchestral texture, but there is no hard edge to its tone. In the Eighth Symphony, Mahler's harps are not only heard alone, rippling gently through the orchestra; but to give bite and incisiveness he doubles the harp and piano on a melodic single line, and thus creates an entirely new effect.

Despite his reputation with his enemies as an uncontrolled and undisciplined Romantic, Mahler never gave mere beauty of sound or sensuousness of effect first priority. His objective was always clarity of expression and while that might sometimes call for richness it could also demand harsh, uncomfortable and even abrasive orchestral writing. This obsession with clarity goes some way to explain the prominence of the voice in his symphonies and, conversely, the unexpected prominence of subtle or grand symphonic effects in his song settings.

Right and on page 88: two scenes from the Netherlands Dance Company's ballet version of the adagio of Mahler's unfinished Tenth Symphony, danced by Sonja van Beers and Billy Wilson Overleaf: Rehearsing Mahler's Sixth Symphony. (Left) cowbells and conductor, (top right) cymbals, (below right) percussionist's eye view

Chapter 8

Building Symphonic Worlds

The 'world' of a Mahler symphony grows out of a wealth of diverse thematic material. Whereas conventional symphonic form presented a first and second subject which were then developed, a Mahler symphony has first and second subject groups of themes. Each group yields several other themes, usually complete melodies which can also be analysed into still further thematic fragments or motifs.

For example, the great orchestral ferment which opens the Second Symphony under a long string tremolo on C is really the source of all the first subject themes of the movement, which Mahler called *Totenfeier* (Ceremony of the Dead). They include the first of several transformations of the *Dies Irae*, the Latin hymn for the dead. All the second subject themes, for their part, seem to grow from a soaring melody first heard in the violins which, in the last movement, after development has given it an unshakeable strength, is associated with Resurrection (the name often given to the whole symphony) and eternal life.

The ideas voiced in the introduction relate the second movement to the first and dominate the finale as well as the long, turbulent *Totenfeier*. The first movement, Mahler explained in the 'programme' of the work which he later suppressed, asks the audience to imagine that it is standing by the coffin of a hero it has loved and followed. What is the value of life, we ask, if it ends in death? Is life only a meaningless, malicious joke? The second subject themes offer some consolation for our loss but no answer to our questions.

The second movement is an Andante, a slow *Ländler* (that Austrian peasants' rural ancestor of the waltz); it is, the composer explained, a happy memory and a sad recollection of lost youth and innocence. In his early symphonies Mahler liked to follow a strenuous, dramatic first movement with one that is lightly scored, but in the Second Symphony this change to a relaxed, gracious and lyrically beautiful move-ment does not mean a mere interlude. As soon as the *Ländler* melody is heard, it repeats itself while the cellos play a beautiful, sadly nostalgic melody against it. Thus the recalled happiness and the sense of loss become one single complex experience and we recognize that the counter-point which conveys it is an essential expressive device and not merely an interesting technique.

Thus far, the Andante has simply offered some relief from the passions of the *Totenfeier*. But in its middle section, a pastoral melody like a nostalgic memory of the Austrian countryside emerges through a passage of gentle though restless triplets which remind the listener of the fierce, disturbing triplet passage in the introduction to the first movement. And now the memory of happiness and the sense of loss have been integrated into the essential meaning of the work.

The scherzo which follows this expresses, according to Mahler, the Hero's disgust and disillusion. It is a brilliant virtuoso orchestral treatment of one of the *Wunderhorn* songs. The movement begins as witty mockery and ends in desperation. It seems to be linked to the symphonic structure only through its train of thought, not musically integrated into the 'world' of the Second Symphony though it belongs psychologically to the experience which that world expresses. A short phrase growing out of the mood of desperation passes by almost incidentally, and it is not until the last move-ment that we learn to understand it as a passionate plea for faith.

A short fourth movement—a setting for contralto and orchestra of a religious poem from *Des Knaben Wunderhorn*—follows the scherzo without a break and leads into the finale. It is a prayer for faith addressed to the Virgin Mary, beginning like a solemn chorale and moving through a passage of passionate pleading to a final, confident faith all in the space of thirty-five bars; this is the real interlude in the symphonic argument, and it is very beautiful and poignantly moving.

It leads, however, to a great orchestral uproar, and sets Mahler off on the only self-confessed piece of orchestral narrative music he ever wrote. The bewildered mourner has experienced gentle sorrow, disillusion and a sense of the worthlessness of humanity, but his questions are not answered. He cannot, knowing them, maintain the radiant faith of *O Röschen rot*. The music is an intensification of ideas heard in the first movement and the cry of faith which failed to prevail in the scherzo becomes more and more passionate. A new theme, a deliberately vulgarized version of the *Dies Irae* converted into a boisterous march, imposes order on the agonized music; the end of the world has come, the graves have opened and their occupants, the great and the small, the kings and the beggars, the saints and the sinners, march to judgement, without dignity or grandeur, without pretensions to nobility or grace. The Last Trumpet peals out; a last nightingale sings softly as it does so.

So much of the work was clear in Mahler's mind when he started to write it in 1887, and by the summer of 1888 it was more or less complete up to the crisis of the Last Trumpet. But when he planned the work, Mahler had felt that, like Beethoven's Ninth Symphony, it must end in some irrefutable affirmation which only words could express, and the words eluded him. He claimed to have ransacked the Bible, European poetry, the writings of eastern mystics and philosophers to find the text he needed, but without success. The work remained incomplete and the Third Symphony was begun before, at Hans von Bülow's funeral in 1894, the choir sang the ode *Resurrection*, by Theodor Klopstock; these words, with a stanza of his own which he added, gave Mahler what he needed. The ode enters in a gentle whisper—'You will arise after a short sleep, O my dust'—the music has the strength and confidence of a chorale; Mahler's own stanza develops and explains the cry of faith which has been working away in the development since the end of the third movement, and Klopstock's words become a thunderous cry of triumph underlined by the strength of the 'Resurrection' theme.

The Second Symphony is a huge work, virtually a concert programme in itself. It includes wide and apparently contradictory experiences and emotions, but Mahler achieves integrity and unity through, rather than in

MAHLER

1860 Born – Kalisch – 1911 – dies Vienna.

Mahler's 1st period consists of symphonies 1-4.

- No 1 in D (1885-8)

Original title TITAN.

Orchestra · large   4 Flutes, oboes + clarinets
                       7 horns
                       4 trumpets
                       2 timpanists

spite of, the variety of ideas he handles. It is possible that lengthy, detailed analysis might prove that the essential themes of the work are simply the *Dies Irae* and the 'Resurrection' theme, and that it is from these that the great, creative turbulence of the introduction is formed. Mahler's themes are capable of remarkable transformations when they are developed, and they are capable of appearing entirely and unrecognizably disguised in several movements.

Thematic transformation was an essential part of his style. 'According to my principle,' he told Natalie Bauer-Lechner, 'there should be no direct repetition. Everything should constantly develop as it goes forward.' Development modifies the themes which are developed, and Mahler gave unity to his huge forms by bringing themes from early movements into later ones, often in forms and disguises so new that only considerable experience of a work enables us to recognize them. The Second Symphony is an intensely exciting experience—'This isn't a Symphony, it's an act of Nature', a student is said to have exclaimed after hearing the work for the first time—but it has its weaknesses. The nightingale which sings during the Last Trumpet seems to be no more than a pretty, poetical idea with no musical importance whatever. For all its length, the Second Symphony achieves an entirely convincing form, whereas the First achieves unity only because it is haunted by the interval of a fourth, which appears in all its themes.

The later symphonies depend more and more on the transformations of a few themes to provide all the material necessary for their movements. To what extent thematic transformation was a conscious technique which Mahler deliberately applied, and to what extent he invented new themes only to discover their sources in a single musical experience (or sometimes, perhaps, not to discover it at all), it is impossible to say. When he had ended the Third Symphony, in which he followed the whole chain of being from inanimate nature through human life and the angels to end with a meditation on love as a manifestation of God, he described the first movement as 'a great laugh for the whole world.' Only gradually does he seem to have realized the outrageous audacity of the movement, a long symphonic march which marvellously suggests the dawning of life into the world and then allows life to

flower into remarkable diversities, startlingly refined, eternally original, grand, picturesque, gentle and almost flamboyantly vulgar. He came to speak of it with not entirely pretended horror as his 'monster'.

He later decided the Symphony was a failure. He had 'dreamed of a great unity of movements that has come to nothing. Each of them is sufficient in itself.' Had the work of integration been a conscious process, he would never have felt this sense of failure. Yet in spite of this, his unconscious seems to have worked more effectively than he realized, for it is possible to see the entire work in relationship to ideas first promulgated in the sprawling, disconcerting first movement. The six-movement Third Symphony was, in its preliminary sketch, a work in seven movements; the Fourth was to be in six movements. In the actual writing, the Fourth symphony shrank to four movements, three purely orchestral and the last the song. Mahler the conscious planner always yielded to Mahler the working composer because the composer achieved more than the planner.

The Fourth Symphony is the shortest and most apparently traditional of all Mahler's works; it demands, according to its title page, a 'small orchestra' though it adds a glockenspiel to a normal percussion section and additional wood-wind and horns; its 'smallness' is simply its lack of trombones. In addition, it lasts for less than forty-five minutes and at first the composer thought of it as a 'symphonic Humoresque'. But it is in a completely symphonic style. It is based on a poem telling of a child's idea of heaven, where the saints and angels are all German folk-tale characters leading simple peasant lives in perfect happiness.

Naturally, the steps by which Mahler reaches this touching naïvety are sophisticated in the extreme. A chatter of wood-wind—some commentators have described the passage as 'farmyard noises' but Mahler said that it is the sound of the sleighbells that carry us to heaven—makes way for a charming, cheerful first subject. The second subject is an almost Schubertian song for the cellos on its first appearance. As these are developed, they create more material, including a flute call high in its register.

The scherzo is one of Mahler's pictures of everyday life, a long wandering *moto perpetuo* type of theme; it is also a dance of death, for

Mahler wrote over it *Freund Heinz spielt an—* 'Death goes on playing'. Death is a solo violin, its strings tuned up a semitone to sound thin and penetrating, like a street player's fiddle, as it threads its way through the *moto perpetuo.* Mahler said that this is a weird, uncanny movement which would make hair stand on end, but it is whimsical and temperamental rather than frightening, and it deals in unusual or apparently incompletely motivated orchestral effects— plucked strings against bowed strings, inexplicable *sforzandi* and strange disturbances of the rhythm. It is laid out in a loose rondo form, with contrasting episodes between restatements of the main theme which, true to Mahler's principles, are never simple repetitions, and its coda modulates from G, the symphony's main key, to E major and gives us a first blissful glimpse of the child's heaven for which we are bound.

The slow movement is a set of double variations on two themes, the first, new to the work, is serene and beautiful, the second is a relation of the first subject of the opening movement, but expressing an anguished yearning that is the work's only unhappy note. The variations grow quicker and increasingly gay, with a dancing glockenspiel leading the fun, and then slip back into the utter tranquillity of the movement's opening before the coda again leaps into E major and the only great *fortissimo* climax the work contains. The gates of heaven open in a blaze of glory and the apparently insignificant flute theme from the first movement becomes the music of heavenly trumpets. After this there comes an ultra-sophisticated simplicity. The sleighbells return, melodic suggestions from the first and second movements come to their fulfilment, and Mahler accepts without any reservations all the quaintnesses of a gilt and gingerbread heaven in which St Martha is the cook, the Apostles look after the sheep and slaughter the lamb for dinner while St Ursula and her companion martyrs make music to which earthly music cannot compare. Never was Mahler so easy-going, so warmly human and so simply happy. But the structure and designs are as firm and strong as those of the fierce, tough, intellectual Second Symphony, or any of Mahler's deliberately powerful works.

To attempt to annotate and describe the processes of cross-reference and thematic transformation by which Mahler unifies the apparent diversities of his symphonies to give each work its integrity of form is, perhaps, inevitably to suggest that his methods are fundamentally crude. The various disguises in which the themes appear from movement to movement are always effective; it is only considerable acquaintance with the music that teaches us how Mahler has really presented a number of aspects of the same experience.

Possibly all the important themes of the grim Sixth Symphony are created by the experience which gave immediate birth to the resolute march theme that sets the work off on its tragic course. The second subject of its first movement is, according to Mahler, a portrait of Alma, colourful, proud and conquering, but it seems to be a remote transformation of the original march, just as the first theme of the symphony's finale can be heard as a new transformation of the Alma theme, no longer proud and conquering but aspiring in spite of wretchedness and sorrow. Whether Mahler heard them in that way or not we do not know, for thematic transformation is one of the topics he did not discuss.

The transformation of the *Dies Irae* into a variety of themes, all of different though related character, in the Second Symphony, the discovery that a new aspect of the sunny theme which opens the Fourth Symphony is full of pain and longing, are anything but obvious; they are not tricks to give a spurious sense of novelty to things that are fundamentally the same. They are the result of a remarkable musical mind of great inventiveness and subtlety considering a subject with a passionate concern which makes technique always one of its less immediate concerns.

One of the more regularly recurring controversies in music is between what is loosely termed 'programme music' and 'absolute' music. The debate centres upon the question as to whether music should, or indeed even can, portray non-musical experiences or intellectual concepts or whether it is merely a matter of sounds and aural stimuli. There are some who believe that 'abstract' music is somehow better than programme music, more pure and more truly music. They may be right, yet almost all music in the nineteenth century was programmatic rather than abstract and it is the nineteenth century that dominates our concert halls today. Mahler in fact had few doubts on the issue. 'Since Beethoven's day, there is no

Mahler conducting Beethoven's Ninth Symphony in Strasbourg, 1905. By this time, his conducting was developing a very great restraint

modern music that does not contain an inner programme,' he wrote in a letter to Max Kalbeck, the critic and translator, and went on, 'But if somebody has to explain to the listener what it means, the music is valueless.'

Mahler, then, accepted the broadly programmatic nature of music in his day and attributed the fact to the influence of Beethoven, but he also saw that the composer was confronted by a problem. The meaning of the music had to be self-evident and the music self explanatory; since if it were not, why use music at all? In a letter to another friend, Max Marschalk, he had said: 'If I were able to put my experience into words, I wouldn't compose music about it. . . . Just as I find it a platitude to write music to illustrate a programme, I find it sterile to give a programme to a completed score.' In the famous last movement of his Ninth Symphony, Beethoven had called on the words of Schiller to enable him to present an entirely specific meaning and by this intrusion of words into the symphonic form had, so Mahler believed, made 'abstract' music impossible. Thereafter composers faced the problem of making their meaning immediately clear to audiences who might have no prior knowledge of their charac-

teristic turns of expression.

He disliked simple 'storytelling' music and the programmes that went with it and believed that even the conventional programme note had become useless—giving an audience the themes of a modern work would only confuse it, for the music of his day was, he wrote, 'too complex to be explained by the notes of a few themes.' Yet despite all this he could not avoid the programmatic conventions of his age and issued his first two symphonies with explanatory programmes. He later discarded them but he did not stop writing programme music in the post-Beethoven sense he had defined.

Mahler believed that his works needed musical understanding. But, recognizing that his style was new and that the diversity of style which he admitted into a work would puzzle the majority of listeners, he decided that he would have to allow the necessity of helping them understand him to override his dislike of literary programmes. He explained to Marschalk:

Having come up eternally against the same misunderstandings and questions, I have come to the opinion that it is just as well if an audience is given a few milestones and pointers for the journey, at least for the time being, while my sort of music seems still strange to them.

Thus the First Symphony appeared with a title, *The Titan*, and a brief title to each of its movements. The title referred not to Greek mythology but to the novel of that name, by Jean-Paul Richter, published in 1803. It is the story of the spiritual and emotional development of a young prince through the influence of the two women he loved, and its distance from the atmosphere of the *Lieder . eines Fahrenden Geselden*, which provided Mahler with a musical starting point, indicate at once that the symphony is not 'about' Richter's novel. Mahler saw the work as a symphony in two parts and, originally, in five movements. Part One, *From the Days of Youth: youth-, fruit-, and thorn pieces*, had originally three movements, *Youth and no end*, *Blumine* (*Flower piece*) and *Full sail*, the scherzo. *Blumine*, a charming intermezzo, he eventually removed and it was forgotten until Benjamin Britten conducted a performance at the Aldeburgh Festival in 1967.

Part Two, called *Commedia Umana*, consists of the slow movement 'Shipwreck and funeral march' and '*Dall' Inferno al Paradiso*; *allegro furioso*; the sudden expression of a deeply wounded heart'. Mahler offered an additional note to the funeral march. The Hunter's Funeral is an engraving by Jacques Callot, the seventeenth-century engraver, familiar to German children as an illustration to a well-known book. The hunter's funeral procession is led by a band of human and animal musicians and followed by animals and birds rejoicing in the departure of their enemy. Musically, it begins as a march in which the children's song, *Frère Jacques*, is played as a canon over drumtaps.

Despite his extension of it, Mahler found one aspect of conventional symphonic form of fundamental value: its use of thematic groups which can be reconciled through development is the central feature of his work. But for him, music and experience are linked, and since experience does not recur in exactly identical forms, neither exact repeats nor precise recapitulations appear in his symphonies. The second time we hear any passage, it is always changed in some way; as if modified by its own earlier experience and by our earlier experience of it. Reprise and recapitulation become stages in the development, not returns to earlier ideas or points at which the argument is drawn to a conclusion. 'According to my principle, there should be no direct repetition; everything should constantly develop as it goes forward.'

For all their apparent explicitness, the titles and sub-titles that Mahler provided for his early works are intended to suggest only states of mind in which the music can best be approached. Mahler often said that the way to understand his latest symphony was from a familiarity with the earlier ones. Only in this way could the hearer develop a feeling for the complexes of themes he used for symphonic subjects; for his unusual orchestration; his readiness to make music out of clichés and cheap, popular tunes and his adjustments and adaptations of traditional forms.

The guide notes to the Second Symphony offered no suggestions of a complexity of vision, but Mahler eventually suppressed them, too. As he wrote the Third, he evolved a series of movement titles, but eventually published the work without them. The first movement is *Pan awakes: Summer marches in:* at one point, the various sections of the huge march had subtitles; one passage, to which Mahler referred when Bruno Walter visited him in Steinbach and he said that he had composed the Höllengebirge, was *What the mountains tell me*. Another passage, which Richard Strauss compared to a Workers' May Day procession, was *The Mob*. The second movement was *What the Flowers in the Meadows tell me*, the third *What the Animals in the Forest tell me*, the fourth, a setting for contralto of a passage from Nietzsche's *Also sprach Zarathustra*, was *What Man tells me*. The fifth movement, a song in which angels assure man that his sins are forgiven, is *What the Morning Bells tell me*; the words are from *Des Knaben Wunderhorn* and the music, for a boy's choir and a women's choir, is marvellously fresh and innocent. The last movement, of beautifully controlled sublimity, is *What Love tells me*. Though Mahler suppressed the titles, he discussed the work in so many letters that they were never a secret.

The Fourth Symphony, when it was first in Mahler's mind, had the same 'milestones and signposts', but when, as he composed it, it apparently changed a good deal of its character, he let the world have it without any adventitious aids. 'I know the most wonderful names for the movements,' he told Natalie Bauer-Lechner, 'but I'm not going to betray them to the rabble

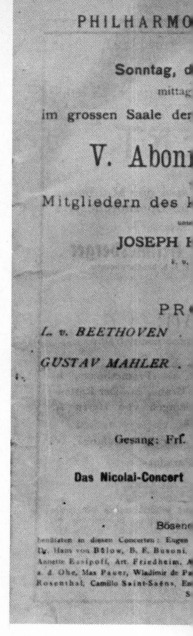

Above: Announcement of the first performance in Vienna of Mahler's Fourth Symphony. The concert ended in fisticuffs

Above right: Mahler studying scores before a concert in Rome

of critics and listeners, so that they, in turn, can betray them to banal misunderstandings and distortions.'

Though the precise connection between the Fourth and the Fifth is anything but clear, the Fifth, Sixth and Seventh Symphonies are a cycle in which certain ideas reappear from work to work.

They are huge works. Number Five is described on its title page as being 'For large Orchestra'; it is scored for four flutes, three of each of the other wood-wind, six horns, four trumpets, bass drum, side drum, cymbals, triangle, gong and glockenspiel as well as strings and harp. The Sixth asks for quadruple wood-wind, eight horns, six trumpets, two sets of timpani, at least two harps, a celeste, or more than one if possible, xylophone, cowbells, a low-pitched bell, a slapstick and a hammer which is used to strike something which makes a dry, unreverberant sound. The Seventh asks for cowbells and xylophone, and in its second movement, *Nachtsmusik*, requires mandoline and guitar.

Together, the three symphonies show a remarkable development of Mahler's style. His mind had always worked in terms of harmony growing out of two or three independent lines of counterpoint, but in the earlier symphonies the implications of this harmony are

sometimes worked out very fully; so that the music has a complex, often very rich, texture. The Fifth Symphony and its successors strip away anything that exists only to cushion the often dissonant lines of melody, and, as a result, the music is frequently bare, harsh and spiky. The composer's aggressive determination to deal in essentials only makes for spare orchestral effects which ensure that those essentials are presented with the greatest possible clarity.

Despite their length, these works are remarkably economical. Everything that happens in the exposition of a movement, even figures which seem at first to be created only as accompaniment, is used as material for development. Furthermore, however contrasted the themes seem to be at their first appearance, they have underlying features in common which become more apparent as the music develops. Mahler extends his technique of cross-reference between movements even more than in the earlier works. Themes may be subjected to complex and startling transformations yet they are nevertheless integrated as the symphony unfolds, so that the musical world which Mahler presents to us, wide ranging as it is in emotions and experiences, proves to be a unity.

The Fifth Symphony, composed in 1901 and

95

1902, contrasts two states of mind. It is in 'three parts' and five movements, part one opening 'with measured tread, sternly, like a funeral march'. But it is a funeral march that accepts the necessity of death; and treads firmly onwards; though its middle section is marked 'With passion. Wild', it is the passion of grief not of rebellion.

The second movement, however, marked 'Stormy, with the greatest vehemence', transforms the theme of the march into a mood of rebellion; though the march itself continues behind the rage, its heavy tread and anguish being heard in moments of relative quietness. A momentary modulation to the key of D major offers a glimpse of hope, and the key returns at the end of the movement in a triumphant chorale-like melody before a coda brings the movement to a close in an anguish of rebellion which has worn itself out. The momentary appearance of the key of D major is important. Many composers have found the mood of this key one of glory and hope and Mahler uses it in the huge scherzo that makes up the second part of the symphony and the finale which is the third part. Thus part one can be seen as a gigantic preparation for the later triumph. Though Mahler never explained the emotional programme underlying his concept of the Fifth, the mood of triumph comes to overwhelm the later part of the work as though expressing, quite simply, the glory of artistic creation. The scherzo which is part two is, from a technical point of view, a symphonic treatment of *Ländler* and waltz rhythms. They proliferate with splendid inventiveness and the melodic phrases escape from the closed rhythm of the dance, striding or gliding across bar lines, as a huge rondo.

Yet, for all its élan, this scherzo is not the final triumph. Perhaps we can see in it a portrayal of the social and working life of the confident master musician, and it is balanced by the short Adagietto, which meditates on withdrawal from the world in terms reminiscent of the song *Ich bin der Welt abhanden gekommen*. This little Adagietto, however, has none of the song's ecstasy; it is, rather, the nostalgic yearnings of the creative mind for a peace which it can never have. The Rondo Finale dispels and at the same time satisfies these yearnings by setting free a passionate creativity that seems to discipline itself within the musical form of the Rondo, rather than to be cast in it by an outside

hand. The main theme and episodes of this rondo are rich in possibilities for symphonic development and even work fruitfully together in terms of academic counterpoint. Mahler shows himself a true master of all the procedures of fugue and canon, yet, while the technique may be academic, the effect is spontaneous.

When one comes to know this movement well, one realizes that startlingly expressive 'new' themes are in fact old themes seen in new aspects. The chorale from the second movement, transformed into bustling geniality, becomes the main theme, and the Adagietto melody, turning from contemplation to activity, reappears. The final triumph is that of music itself, announced as the chorale melody in a new, glorious form, which grows grandly out of the whirl of activity.

The Sixth Symphony was completed in 1904. Like the Fifth, it shows a fine balance between intellectual mastery and intensity of emotion. However there is one major formal point that Mahler himself never finally resolved and that is the relative positions of the grim, sarcastic, painful scherzo and the beautiful slow movement. This latter movement is the only offer of ease and peace in the whole work and the composer could not decide whether it should come before the scherzo as the second movement or after it as the third. Two published versions, each authorized by Mahler, show the movement in the two alternative positions.

Mahler called the Sixth his 'Tragic' Symphony; it is fierce, harshly scored music, which fights a desperate war against sorrow and ends in profound despair. Mahler had more to say on the work to his biographer, Richard Specht. 'My Sixth, will represent riddles to the solution of which only a generation which has previously absorbed and understood my first five symphonies will have the courage to apply itself.' Both Mahler and his wife saw the work as intensely personal; its first movement is a resolute, persistent march. The second group themes grow out of a proudly soaring melody which, according to the composer, was a musical portrait of his wife. These themes struggle towards happiness only to be crushed three times by a chord of A major which is depressed into A minor and followed by a disconsolate woodwind chorale. The chord itself, and the drum rhythm which accompanies it, act as a motto theme to the entire symphony. Cowbells, their sound apparently drifting up-

Right: The house in Vienna in
which Mahler lived from 1907
to 1910
Below: Mahler at leisure
during his New York season
of 1910

wards to a solitary climber, offer the only relief from struggle.

In the scherzo, Mahlerian dance themes are tormented into alien rhythms, so that their movement becomes unnatural and puppet-like. An apparently unimportant cadence theme from the first movement becomes a cry of angry pain. The trio marked 'old-fashioned' is happier—but it is swept away by the return of the scherzo. Alma Mahler saw in the movement a prophecy of the fate of their elder daughter, as though its movement, sometimes eager, sometimes reluctant, always rhythmically dubious, were the ungainly movements of a toddler, and she was terrified to hear them stumble into silence.

The slow movement is a beautiful, lyrical, pastoral Andante which offers escape from tragedy but no solution to the problems of the work, and the finale is one of Mahler's most remarkable movements, cast in sonata form with a slow introduction. The main theme of the first group is an aspiring, yearning version of the Alma melody of the first movement which seems to have forgotten its function as portraiture. The rest of the themes are transformations of melodies heard in the first movement and the scherzo, and the exposition is brought to an end by one of Mahler's most remarkable effects—the sound of a hammer striking a single blow; Mahler demanded that the sound it produced be dead, dry, unresonant, not metallic. Even after this the music struggles on with desperate hope, the themes producing new transformations which bring them nearer in character to each other and to the determined march theme that opened the work. The development is long, and aggressive; then the hammer stroke crushes it again. The recapitulation goes on, still struggling for an impossible happiness, and originally ended in the third hammer blow. 'The hero suffers three blows of fate,' Mahler explained. 'The third fells him like an ox.' In later versions the third blow was omitted, but even without it the hero is annihilated; the music reaches a final climax and the brass make a fugal passage out of the tragic chorale of the first movement. Another chord roars out and dies into silence.

To Mahler the music was an entirely personal statement. Three years later, when his daughter died, Vienna rejected him and his fatal heart disease was diagnosed, he saw it as a prophecy of his own fate. But the music is more than a private statement and transcends its creator. It belongs to the world we are too familiar with, of mechanical, empty frivolities, the collapse of empires, war, horror and death. Perhaps, the work is personal only in so far as Mahler's tragedy epitomises the tragedy of our age.

The Seventh Symphony, though it contains splendid music, is probably the least satisfactory of all Mahler's works. Its second and fourth movements, both called *Nachtsmusik* (Serenade) were composed in 1904. The first, third and fifth movements were composed in 1905, and though the scherzo, marked 'shadowy', shares the nocturnal mood, the first movement seems to belong to a different area of experience, and the attempt to triumph through artistic creativity in another Rondo Finale fails because, for the only time in a symphony, Mahler seems to be looking hard for appropriate themes and constructing a suitable movement instead of exploring ideas and finding their form as he does so.

It seems that the Seventh left Mahler doubting its effectiveness and even his own inspiration, but in the summer of 1906 he found himself possessed by music for the Latin hymn, *Veni, Creator Spiritus* ('Come Holy Ghost, our souls inspire'). This music led him to an inspired vision of the last scene of Goethe's *Faust*, in which the hero is carried up into heaven. In eight weeks Mahler sketched the whole gigantic work which was to be the Eighth Symphony and within a year had finished its scoring. It had its first performance in Munich in 1910, announced, to its composer's fury, as 'The Symphony of the Thousand' on account of its vast forces. It requires: quintuple wood-wind, eight horns, four trumpets, four trombones, organ, piano, celeste, two harps, glockenspiel, a battery of other percussion, strings and an offstage band of four trumpets and three trombones. Eight solo singers and a double choir built to balance his orchestra, with an extra boy's choir large enough to be heard against all the other performers, make it the largest of all his colossal works.

The first movement is an orthodox symphonic first movement with two contrasted subjects, a long development section, a Mahlerian recapitulation which continues the development and a coda, all worked out with blazing intensity and dominating technical mastery. The cry for love and wisdom, *Accende*

Mahler on the way to New York in 1910

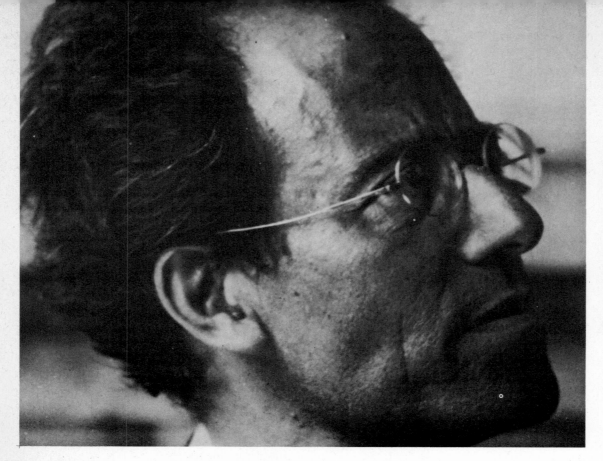

*Left: Mahler as director of the
Vienna Imperial Opera
Above: Mahler in Amsterdam,
1906*

lumen sensibus ('Enlighten our minds') becomes
an even greater climax, with every one of the
performers except the offstage band contri-
buting rather than simply adding weight to the
clamour, so that one is conscious of power rather
than of noise.

The second movement is a loose, often lyrical,
often rhapsodic symphonic drama, very different from the taut structural power of the
triumphal march in Part One. The contrast in
style is a deliberate part of the composer's
design, for Part Two is really the musical
consequence of Part One and its psychological
fulfilment. It is the redemption of the Faustian
spirit in every man, by divine inspiration.

A long *adagio* passage of mountain music,
lonely and serenely impassioned, portrays hermits praying in solitude. Two themes develop—
a pizzicato bass from cellos and double basses,
and a melody that passes from instrument to
instrument above it and is treated sparely but
polyphonically; the two themes sound quite
unlike each other, but each is a transformation
of the *Accende lumen sensibus* melody of the
first movement. Little Angels, Mahler's boys'
choir, carry Faust's soul aloft to a new melody,
graceful, innocent and charming, which is yet

another transformation of *Accende lumen
sensibus*. The nearer we are to the heart of
heaven, the richer and more freely emotional
the music becomes until at last we are face to
face with the Blessed Virgin. The final words
were headed by Goethe with the words
'*Chorus Mysticus*'. They celebrate the realities
of heaven after the illusions and symbols of
earthly existence. It is announced as a whisper
but becomes triumphant, gloriously and ir-
resistibly powerful, as its melody, the final
transformation of the *Accende* theme, unites
with the melody of the *Mater Gloriosus*. To
this, the offstage brass adds the theme of the
opening *Veni Creator*. For Mahlerians, the
gates of heaven are opened.

The first performance of the work was
Mahler's one undisputed triumph; there were
no dissenters; a crowded audience accepted it,
was deeply moved and cheered Mahler to the
echo. The size of the work, of course, is moving
in itself; the power he unharnesses is almost
irresistible, and its masterly control and integration of its huge thematic apparatus— the
triumph of a natural, instinctive, musical
architect—almost defies the listener to reject
its message.

Chapter 9

The Music of Farewell

The events of 1907—his daughter's death, his departure from Vienna and the diagnosis of his fatal heart disease—created a new Mahler, a bitter, rebellious composer grasping more eagerly for life as death approached.

His moods oscillated between bitter, angry depression and feverish gaiety. It was only in music that he managed to cope with life: in music, too, he learnt to cope with the idea of death.

In the summer of 1908 he began to write *Das Lied von der Erde*, 'The Song of the Earth'. The idea for the work seems to have been in his mind since he had been given a translated anthology of ancient Chinese poetry a year before. He was attracted by lyrics attributed to Li-Tai-Po, in which desperate pessimism blends with a love of natural beauty and a delight in wine and its effects. Mahler had begun to set some of these as independent songs before he realized that a major work was taking shape. It became 'A symphony in six movements for contralto (or baritone) tenor and orchestra.'

But although it was to all intents and purposes a true symphony, the three short central songs together forming as it were the scherzo of a four movement work, Mahler did not number it as such. To do so, he seems to have thought would have been to tempt providence. He felt the Sixth Symphony as a prophecy of his own destruction, the death of his daughter seemed to him the fulfilment of a prophecy in the *Kindertotenlieder* and both Bruckner and Beethoven had died after the completion of their ninth symphonies. Only when the *Song of the Earth* was complete and fate had, so to speak, been cheated did Mahler embark on what he called his 'ninth' symphony.

According to an orthodox analysis, the main key of the *Song of the Earth* is C minor but the main themes of the work use the pentatonic or five-note scale of Chinese music so that the key structure is often discounted. The first movement sets out the emotional premises of the whole work. It is entitled *Trinklied vom Jammer der Erde*, 'The drinking song of the Earth's Sorrow' and is set for solo tenor. A party is about to get under way but the voice solo insists that before they begin the serious drinking the guests hear him out as he delivers an impassioned lament on the transient nature of life's joys. Life is laid waste by sorrow and, while natural beauty, wine, friendship and music may offer brief consolations, the reality of things mocks us like an ape gibbering derisively at us from a tombstone. The pentatonic main theme is almost yelled at the audience by the trumpet as the work opens, and taken up by the strings. The thought of sky and cloud brings a melody of great beauty, but each stanza ends with the refrain—'Life is dark, and so is death' screwed up by a semitone at each return. The phantom ape gibbering in its churchyard at human hope forces the singer to howl into the wild orchestral uproar. Possibly Mahler, the great reviser and retoucher, might have lessened the singer's problems if he had heard the work in performance, but he was a long-experienced and practical composer fully capable of judging the effect in the score and the passage as it stands certainly expresses the horror and intensity of his feelings.

The mood changes for the second song, *Der Einsame in Herbst* (The lonely one in Autumn). Over a murmuring, wandering viola figure and a mournful, pentatonic melody on the oboe the contralto sings longingly of death as an ending to loneliness. The autumn mist mentioned in the poem's first lines is vividly conjured up and all is beautiful, restrained and sad. The next two songs, the tenor's *Von der Jugend* and the contralto's *Von der Schönheit* ('On Youth' and 'On Beauty') change the mood to speak of the consolations of life. In a little pavilion on a lake, reached by a high-curved bridge, friends sit and drink tea together; they are elegant, witty and young. The music gleams, it is light and relaxed and exotically charming; a little breeze flutters the glassy surface of the lake, but storm and trouble are forgotten. The contralto's hymn in praise of beauty is more intense and rises to a fierce and rapturous climax. The scene opens on a group of girls, picking flowers by the banks of a lake. A troop of young horsemen careers past, the hooves of their horses crushing the flowers; as they gallop away into the distance, one of the girls stands looking lovingly after the strongest and handsomest of them.

After these brief happy interludes, the music darkens with cynical, hollow merriment in the fifth song—again for tenor—*Der Trunkener in Fruhling*, 'The Drunkard in Spring'. 'As life is only a dream, I spend my life drinking myself into a stupor. I woke up this morning to discover that spring had come, but what have I to do with Spring? I want to be drunk again.' The consolations of beauty, love, poetry and

Scene from The Song of the Earth, *Kenneth Macmillan's ballet version of* Das Lied von der Erde, *danced by the Royal Ballet*

Scene from The Song of the
Earth

friendship have failed; drink offers the comforts of insensibility. This concludes the three-part 'scherzo' of this unnumbered symphony; brief episodes of spring music have been challenged and overcome by drunken pessimism. Throughout, the basic pentatonic theme has flowered into variant melodies, but the integrity of the work has been established by methods that Mahler had employed in all his earlier symphonies.

The last movement, *Der Abschied* ('The Farewell'), sums up the entire work. Beauty, love and friendship are recalled in music of great intensity, only to be dismissed. The words are an assembly of two poems, by two other Chinese poets—a song of a man waiting at sunset to bid farewell to a friend and one in which two friends part for ever. After the first has gone, explaining that his life has been hard, the second wanders into the mountains awaiting his own hour of departure. To this, Mahler added words of his own to provide the text for his coda: always, everywhere, the world renews itself and its beauty in spring: always, everywhere, the distance shines, alluring, blue and bright.

The music is a long, beautifully shaped sonata-form movement. There are three main themes. The first is a free and improvisatory melody for the oboe; it goes through many transformations and, at the climax of the development section, its tail-piece provides material for a short but magnificent funeral march. The second is a group of themes unfolded as the singer waits at sunset for his friend; sleep, with its illusion of happiness, is coming over the world. The third theme describes the beauty of evening, and it grows out of the theme in the first song which saluted the beauty of the world. The movement is spacious and leisurely. At times the voice runs in free recitative under the barest possible treatment of the oboe melody; at times it shapes a melody as the text demands lyrical expression. As always when Mahler is at his greatest and most intense, the music seems to be less a form than a continuous train of thought, although the form is in reality precise and strongly built. The parting of the friends is a compressed recapitulation which shows the themes in a new, more intense, light and allows Mahler to reach his own unique mood of heart-broken calm.

The ending of the work is, for the Mahler-lover, a long and beautiful miracle. The key of C minor re-establishes itself as though for the conclusion, but then lifts itself into C major for a coda in which the contralto sings a beautiful transformation of the melody that has symbolized natural beauty throughout the work. It is accompanied by the orchestra at its most delicately evocative and refined, with celeste, mandoline and harp making exotic, magical sounds. The music dies away on the singer's repetitions of the last word, *ewig* ('forever'), while the original pentatonic theme, inverted, attempts to climb to an unattainable fulfilment, repeating itself as the contralto does. The final sound is a dissonance; the cadence which might end the work is never completed, as though the music itself would merge into eternity.

The Ninth Symphony is quite consciously Mahler's Farewell. The first movement ends with the woodwinds playing a direct quotation from Beethoven's Piano Sonata, opus 81a, which the composer had written for his patron Archduke Rudolph, forced to leave Vienna, and which he had named *Les Adieux*. Mahler's intention is about as explicit as music could make it, but he strengthened the effect still further by introducing the quotation with a passage for solo flute at the top of its register marked 'Very hesitant'. The movement grows from three themes: one is in popular Viennese idiom, reminiscent of a popular song, *Mein Mutter was ein' Wienerin*, and seems to suggest at times a Viennese mother singing a lullaby after showing her young son the beloved city; the bulk of the second group is taken up by a wild, disconsolate melody; and this leads the way to a trumpet theme which culminates in a short fanfare, as the development begins, with a beautifully wistful modification of the main theme. Mahler wrote over the score of his completed sketch 'Oh, vanished days of youth, oh, scattered loves.'

The two themes do not really begin to work together, though they interrupt each other, until the recapitulation. There are no movement titles or sub-headings but it is easy to feel that the music presents the struggle between the hope of peace in eternal sleep and the passionate, bitter, painful fact of life, full of wild terrors and longings. The second subject dissolves into a number of motives each of which is transformed into new shapes; their freely inter-weaving counterpoint leads to anguished harmonic clashes. A funeral march passage provides a few bars of hopelessness before Beethoven's farewell motto slips into the texture of the movement.

The second movement is a scherzo made out of a rustic *Ländler* ('very clumsy and firm' is the direction in the score), a waltz freely treated and finally a slow *Ländler*. Mahler's title for the third movement is *Rondo Burlesque* and on the sketch score he wrote 'To my Brothers in Apollo', but the music is bitingly sarcastic, intellectually savage and tough.

The first movement of the Ninth is explicitly a farewell, indentifying its mood; but there is little of valediction about the second and third movements, with the urgent activity and the brutal, noisy sarcasm of the Rondo Burlesque. In the last movement, Mahler manages to regain the state of heart-broken, resigned serenity in which *The Song of the Earth* ended. The music moves beyond anger and suffering, as though the act of composition had transformed the composer.

The atmosphere of acceptance in which the Ninth Symphony ends was something won through music and existing only in music. It is always hard to link Mahler's music with the actual events and experiences of life, but his work on the Tenth belongs to 1910, when it seemed to him that his marriage was crumbling just as his health and his position in Vienna had crumbled. He died before it was completed. The Tenth Symphony was to be purely orchestral and to have five movements; the first, *Andante* leading to *Adagio*, was complete; the third movement, *Purgatorio* was complete in a sketch but not orchestrated, and the rest of the movements existed only in short-score sketches. In 1924 Alma Mahler allowed a facsimile of all the Tenth Symphony notes and sketches to be published. Immediately the composer Ernst Křenek prepared a performing edition of the first movement and *Purgatorio*.

The first movement is strange, bony, questing music growing out of a long melody for solo viola; it seems to inhabit an emotional world entirely its own without any reference to general experience. The sketch score is pathetically, almost tragically, marked with comments and doodles; the scherzo type movement that was originally planned to be the first but which eventually found its place as fourth carries several of these: 'The devil dances with me.' 'Madness takes hold of me, accursed one. . . .' 'Destroy me, that I may forget that I exist.' 'That I may cease to be, that I. . . .' The *Purgatorio*

movement, originally planned to come second, carries among others the words: 'Have mercy, Lord, why hast though forsaken me?' 'Thy will be done.'

The fourth and fifth movement sketches carry several messages to Alma. They had witnessed a funeral procession in New York which had been signalled by a single stroke on a muffled drum; this drum beat became symbolic to the composer and appears in the score; over it Mahler scrawled to Alma, 'You alone know.' Over the last movement he wrote 'Farewell, my lyre.' In many of his letters to her, Alma is addressed as his lyre. The music is exploratory, resourceful, intellectual as well as emotional, but the battle for serenity, won in *The Song of the Earth* and the Ninth Symphony, had to be fought all over again. The viola solo of the first movement evolves into terror and culminates in a discord on the way to a serene recapitulation. *Purgatorio* is a scherzo; it has a *moto perpetuo* foundation of the type which in earlier works seemed to symbolize earthly life, and it has no terrors. Possibly the title was one of those which Mahler would later have decided to suppress.

To Schoenberg, Berg and the younger generation of Austrian musicians who knew him, Mahler was a musical Moses, leading them from

Left: Arnold Schoenberg in 1910
Above: Mahler's grave in the cemetry in Grinzing, in the suburbs of Vienna

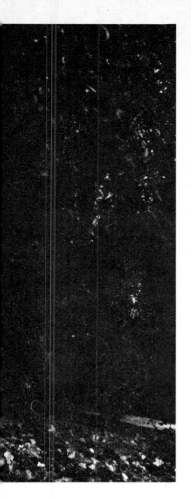

the desert of an exhausted style into a promised land of renewed fruitfulness. For his highly organized, often disturbingly dissonant, use of polyphony and counterpoint suggested a way beyond the Wagnerian exhaustion.

The 'progressive', exploratory Mahler, on whom critics and historians have concentrated their attention, is the essential link between Wagner and Schoenberg. But it is rather doubtful to what extent Mahler would have recognized himself in this description; his technical ability, his co-ordination of masses of material in elaborate symphonic forms, is unparalleled —whatever view a critic, musician or listener takes of the concepts Mahler chose to communicate, his power of communication is something definite, analysable and therefore undeniable—but he thought of himself neither as a 'traditionalist' nor as a 'progressive' but simply as a composer born with the duty of communicating certain experiences through music.

Emphasis on the 'progressive' aspects of Mahler's work seems to obscure his relationship to the composers of his own period. Elgar, born in 1857, Delius, born in 1862, and Richard Strauss, born in 1864, are the Mahler generation and they are linked to him by affinities of spirit and experience if not by technique.

Mahler's extremes of emotion can embarrass or infuriate the unsympathetic. Yet one critic accused Elgar of hysterical emotionalism, sensationalism and sentimentality in terms which, if the name Elgar were omitted, could be mistaken for one of the many attacks on Mahler. Like Mahler, Elgar found symphonic uses for the march, not only in the four *Pomp and Circumstance* marches, but also in movements like the Scherzo of the First Symphony, which uses a determined march for its trio, and in the *Larghetto* funeral march of the Second Symphony, a marvellously hushed ceremonial lamentation.

Affinities between the two composers go to greater depths than this. In 1914, Elgar wrote a piece for strings, harp and organ, *Sospiri*; its instrumentation at once suggests the world of the *Adagietto* for harp and strings in Mahler's Fifth Symphony. Elgar's piece—a very intense, beautiful and moving miniature is not, like Mahler's, rich in closely woven polyphony, but the listener can hardly avoid the thought that *Sospiri* is almost Mahler's *Adagietto* in inversion; Mahler's melody aspires and falls

back, rises again and is again frustrated, so that it reaches always for something beyond its power. Elgar's melody is a very similar curve, it curves downwards, trying to avoid despair but always falling closer to utter desolation.

Delius was a singularly isolated composer with, by the time he reached maturity, only the slightest interest in the music of other men. In *Sea Drift*, composed in 1903, he set a poem by Walt Whitman; the heart of it is the lament of a sea bird which, having lost his mate and failed to call her back to him, remembers their past life and ends with the words 'We two together no more.' The final 'No more' is repeated, whispering, dying away in a texture that, like the end of *The Song of the Earth*, seems slowly and magically to dissolve rather than come to an end.

At the time that Mahler was working on the Eighth Symphony, Delius was composing *The Mass of Life*, the only one of his works which can be described as, or attempted to be, monumental. Its text is from Nietzsche's *Also sprach Zarathustra*, the poetic-philosophical masterpiece which Mahler and Delius both loved. Delius ended *The Mass of Life* with 'Zarathustra's Midnight Song', the concluding lines of which Mahler had set for contralto in the fourth movement of his Third Symphony, as an account of the duality of human experience, the struggle between soy and sorrow. To Delius, these words are a hymn to joy, because joy is stronger, in Delius' view of Nietzsche's words, than any grief. *The Mass of Life* reaches an ecstatic jubilant conclusion and, it, must be admitted, has nothing Mahlerian in the shape of its themes or the layout of its score; nevertheless, *The Mass of Life* ends with rapturously arching vocal phrases which are very close in mood to the final ecstasy of the Eighth Symphony.

Delius loved mountains as Mahler loved them, and both *The Song of the High Hills* and the opening of the second part of *The Mass of Life* paint mountain landscapes not unlike that inhabited by hermits and anchorites in Part Two of Mahler's Eighth Symphony. But Mahler and Elgar both found a special power in traditional musical forms, so that the two Elgar symphonies both reach their final splendour—and the end of his Second Symphony is one of the most glorious sunsets in music—by validly fulfilling the requirements of symphonic form, just as the greatest Mahlerian triumphs are really the triumph of form and tonality over musically disruptive elements.

Mahler himself drew attention to his affinity with Richard Strauss, for all his distrust of Strauss's interest in money and the frivolity which, to Mahler, was incomprehensible. They were both, as in their very different ways were Elgar and Delius, masters of the orchestra, but Mahler's orchestra is far leaner and more austere. Occasionally, Mahler and Strauss seem very close; in its orchestral dress, Strauss's *Morgen* (one of the loveliest of his songs) is a blood relation of Mahler's *Rückert Lieder*. Strauss's *Tod und Verklärung* achieves a triumph over death that comes from the world of the 'resurrection' music of Mahler's Second Symphony. In most of Strauss's music, the composer excuses his intensities and sensationalisms by attributing them to somebody else— Don Juan, Don Quixote, Salome, Baron Ochs, the Marschallin, the young composer of *Ariadne auf Naxos* or 'a Hero'. Mahler was not an opera composer or a writer of symphonic poems because he was incapable of wearing disguises and externalizing his emotions. Strauss went on writing beautiful music until shortly before his death in 1948, and at the end of his life he spoke for himself in the *Four Last Songs*, written from the world of Mahler's Rückert Songs, with rhapsodically free melodies arching gloriously above a disciplined, small, radiant orchestra. It was Strauss who rationalized Mahler's restrained later conducting technique in a series of humorous commands to the conductor and asserted his closeness to Mahler by demanding that *Salome* should be played 'like Chamber music'.

Elgar, Strauss, Delius and Mahler lived in the same world, looked for the same qualities in life and experienced many similar moods. In all their music is the consciousness of living at the end of an age. Elgar to all intents and purposes ended his work in 1918 with the Cello Concerto, bidding farewell to a world that had died before him. Delius, blind and riddled with disease dictated his *Songs of Farewell* with amazing determination, and died with almost flamboyant courage. Strauss, a war later, reached a calm plateau of acceptance with *Am Abendroth* and *Beim schlafengehen*; it is sunset, he sings, and time to sleep. Mahler was mistaken when he thought his music began and ended with himself and his own mind and experience. In the angers, ecstasies and sorrows

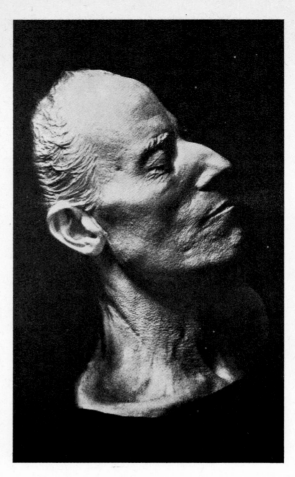

Left: Mahler's death mask
Top: Frederick Delius in 1929, by Augustus John
Above: Edward Elgar

of his work, he seems to be bewailing not only the transience of Gustav Mahler but the passing of the world into which he had been born and had worked. These were preoccupations shared by most artists of his generation; they knew their world was ending.

In 1933, W. B. Yeats wrote of himself and his friends:

We were the last Romantics,—chose for theme
Traditional sanctity and loveliness;
Whatever's written in what poet's name
The book of the people; whatever most can bless
The mind of man or elevate rhyme.

The words apply to Elgar, Delius, Strauss and Mahler. It is part of the melancholy which at moments they all share and which invades their music; they were a good-bye, a sunset. But Mahler could look into the future and write his way into it; he became not only the elegist of a dying world but a prophet of the new world which succeeded it. He belongs to the disciples of the revolution as well as to the heroes of the past.

His life in brief

1860 Mahler born, July 7, at Kalisch
1864 Learns to play folk tunes and marches on the accordion
1866 First piano lessons
1868 First piano pupil, a boy aged seven
1870 First public concert, at Iglau
Pupil of Grünewald, in Prague
1875 Death of his brother Ernst. Admitted to Vienna Conservatoire
1876 Prize for piano playing
1877 Prize for piano playing. Composition prize for Piano Quartet
1880 Conductor at Summer Theatre, Bad Hall
1881 Conductor at the theatre in Ljubljana
1883 Conductor at Olmutz, appointed January. Second Conductor, Court Theatre, Cassel, appointed in June
1885 Conducts Music Festival at Cassel. Appointed Second conductor, Deutsches Theatre, Prague, in August
1886 Second conductor, under Arthur Nikisch, Leipzig
1887 Deputises for Nikisch during Nikisch's illness. Appointed Director of Royal Opera, Budapest, in October
1888 Death of Father (February) and Mother (October). First performance (Budapest) of First Symphony
1891 Leaves Budapest in March. Appointed First Conductor, Stadttheater, Hamburg, in April
1892 Conducts German Opera season (with a mainly Hamburg company) at Covent Garden
1894 First Symphony performed at the Festival of the *Deutsche Allgemeiner Musikverein* in Weimar
1895 Richard Strauss conducts first three movements of the Second Symphony in Berlin. Mahler conducts the entire work there in December
1896 Conducts *Lieder eines fahrenden Gesellen* and First Symphony in Berlin
1897 Conducts in Moscow. Conversion to Catholicism. Appointed Kapellmeister, Vienna Opera, in May. Promoted to Director in October
1898 Conductor, Vienna Philharmonic Concerts. Performances of First and Second Symphonies in Dresden and Liège
1900 Second Symphony performed in Munich. Conducts Vienna Philharmonic in Paris
1901 First performance of *Das Klagende Lied*, Vienna. Breaks with Philharmonic Concerts. First performance of Fourth Symphony, Munich. Meets Alma Maria Schindler, aged 23
1902 First performance of Fourth Symphony in Vienna. Marriage to Alma Maria Schindler, February. First performance of Third Symphony. Birth of elder daughter, Maria, in November
1903 Conducts his symphonies in Basle and Amsterdam. Other performances in Darmstadt and Dusseldorf
1904 First performance of Fifth Symphony, Cologne. Birth of younger daughter, Anna, in June
1906 First performance of Sixth Symphony, Essen
1907 Death of daughter, Maria Anna. Heart disease diagnosed. Resignation from Vienna Opera
1908 First Season at New York Metropolitan Opera. First performance of Seventh Symphony, Prague
1909 Appointed Musical Director, New York Philharmonic Society. Conducts Seventh Symphony in Amsterdam
1910 Conducts first performance of Eighth Symphony, in Munich. Conducts Second Symphony in Paris
1911 Collapses after concert in New York, February 21. Returns to Europe. Dies in Vienna, May 18. First performance of *Das Lied von der Erde*, Vienna, under Bruno Walter
1912 First performance of Ninth Symphony, under Walter
1924 Performance of (two complete movements of) Tenth Symphony
1961 Performance of Tenth Symphony as completed by Deryck Cooke
1972 First Performance of Cooke's revised version of Tenth Symphony

Catalogue of works

1878–80 *Das Klagende Lied*, libretto by the composer. Revised 1888, 1896, 1898. Published 1899
Pre-1884 *Lieder und Gesänge aus der Jugendzeit*, voice and piano. Texts by Tirso del Molinari, Mahler and from *Des Knaben Wunderhorn*. Published: Book One, 1885; Books Two and Three, 1892
1883–5 *Lieder eines fahrenden Gesellen*, voice and orchestra. Text by the composer. Revised 1896. Published 1897
1884–8 First Symphony (*The Titan*). Published 1898
1887–94 Second Symphony (*Resurrection*). Published 1898
1888–?95 *Lieder aus 'Des Knaben Wunderhorn'*, voice and orchestra. Published 1905
1893–6 Third Symphony. Published 1898
1899 *Revelge* and *Der Tamboursg'sell*, voice and orchestra. Texts from *Des Knaben Wunderhorn*. Published 1905
1899–1900 Fourth Symphony. Published 1901. Revised 1910, revision unpublished
1901–4 Fifth Symphony. Published 1904. Repeatedly revised, 1907–9
1901–4 *Kindertotenlieder*, voice and orchestra. Text by Friedrich Rückert. Published 1905
1901–3 *Fünf Lieder nach Rückert*, voice and orchestra. Published 1905
1903–5 Sixth Symphony. Published (two versions, changing order of inner movements) 1906
1904–5 Seventh Symphony. Published 1908
1906–7 Eighth Symphony. Texts: *Veni Creator Spiritus* and final scene from *Faust* by Goethe. Published 1910
1907–8 *Das Lied von der Erde*, Symphony for Contralto (or Baritone) and Tenor. Texts selected from *Die Chinesische Flöte*. Published posthumously, 1911
1909–10 Ninth Symphony. Published posthumously, 1912
1910 Tenth Symphony; two movements complete, the rest in sketch form. Published in facsimile, 1924. Completed by Deryck Cooke, 1961; revised 1972

Bibliography

Adler, G. *Gustav Mahler* (Vienna, 1920)
Aldrich, R. *Concert Life in New York, 1903–23* (New York, 1941)
Barford, P. *Mahler Symphonies and Songs* (London, 1970)
Bauer-Lechner, N. *Erinnerungen an Gustav Mahler* (Vienna, 1923)
Bekker, P. *Gustav Mahlers Sinfonien* (Berlin, 1921)
Blaukopf, K. *Gustav Mahler* (Vienna, 1969)
Bülow, H. von and Strauss, R. (W. Schuh and F. Trennen, eds., translated by A. Gishford) *Correspondence* (London, 1953)
Cardus, N. *Gustav Mahler: his mind and his Music* (London, 2nd Impression, 1972)
Cooke, D. *Gustav Mahler* (London, 1960)
De Lagrange, H. *Mahler Vol I* (London, 1974)
Engel, C. *Gustav Mahler: Song-Symphonist* (New York, 1953)
Graf, M. *Die Wiener Oper* (Vienna, 1955)
Kennedy, M. *Mahler* (Master Musicians) (London 1974)
Mahler, A. (translated by B. Creighton, Introduction by D. Mitchell) *Memories and Letters* (London, 2nd Edition, 1968)
Mahler, G. (A. Mahler, ed.) *Briefe* (Vienna, 1925)
Mitchell, D. *Gustav Mahler: The Early Years* (London, 1958)
Mueller, J. H. *The American Symphony Orchestra* (London, 1958)
Newlin, D. *Bruckner, Mahler, Schoenberg* (New York, 1947)
Prawy, M. *The Vienna Opera* (London, 1969)
Redlich, H. *Bruckner and Mahler* (London, 1955)
Reich, W. *Gustav Mahler in Eigenen Wort—im Worte der Freunde* (Zürich, 1958)
Walter, B. (translated by Lotte Walter Lindt) *Gustav Mahler* (London, 1958)
Wooldridge, D. *The Conductor's World* (London, 1970)

Index

The publishers would like to thank
the following contributors for the use
of their material

Archiv Richard Wagner 49t
Covent Garden Archives 53, 102/3,
  104
Decca half-title page, 9, 100l
Federico Arborio Mella, Milan 36
Fr. Lometsch Verlag Kassel 43
Gesellschaft der Freunde der
  Albertina 17
Hamburgische Staatsoper 51b
John Hillelson Agency 57, 58, 75
Historischen Museums der Stadt
  Wien 65t
Houston Rogers 80/1, 82, 83
Keystone Press Agency 18t and b
Mansell Collection 79, 108t, 108b
Raymond Mander and Joe Mitchenson
  Theatre Collection 12t
Metropolitan Opera Archives 70, 71,
  48
Ost.Nationalbibliothek title page, 15tr,
  22, 24, 27tl, 27tr, 28, 29b, 30r, 31,
  32l, 39b, 42, 43, 44, 56, 60, 60/1,
  61tl, 61tr, 61bl, 61br, 62/3, 64t,
  68/9
Particam Pictures, Amsterdam 85, 88
Staatsbibliothek, Berlin 30l, 52, 106
Stadtarchiv, München 72b
Ullstein Bilderdienst 90, 98
Reg Wilson 45

All other material is the property of
the publishers